ts Politics

The Sociology of Grass Roots Politics

A STUDY OF PARTY MEMBERSHIP

David Berry
LECTURER IN SOCIOLOGY
UNIVERSITY COLLEGE, CARDIFF

MACMILLAN
ST MARTIN'S PRESS

© David Berry 1970

First published 1970 by
MACMILLAN AND CO LTD
Little Essex Street London W C 2
and also at Bombay Calcutta and Madras
Macmillan South Africa (Publishers) Pty Ltd Johannesburg
The Macmillan Company of Australia Pty Ltd Melbourne
The Macmillan Company of Canada Ltd Toronto
St Martin's Press Inc New York
Gill and Macmillan Ltd Dublin

Library of Congress catalog card no. 77-84181

Printed in Great Britain by
WILLIAM CLOWES AND SONS LIMITED
London and Beccles

To My Mother and Father

Contents

List of Tables   9

Preface   11

1 Political Participation and Democracy   13

Theoretical Perspective, 17
American Theory and British Society: the relevance of class conflict, 25
Summary and Preview of the Empirical Study, 29

2 The Approach to Empirical Analysis: Procedure and Community Structure   31

Procedure, 31
Walton Constituency and Church Ward, 34

3 Political Activity and Social Participation   41

Party Activities, 42
Trade Union and Church Memberships, 47
Voluntary Association Activities, 53
Party Divisions and Social Participation, 61

4 Party Divisions and Social Class   65

Occupational Class, 68
Education and Housing, 73
Party Divisions and Political Attitudes, 80

5 Politics, Communications and Social Attitudes   89

Opinion Leadership: interpersonal communication channels, 90
Newspapers, Radio and Television: mass communication channels, 93
Authoritarian Attitudes, 103

6 Theory and Problems of Grass Roots Politics   111

Empirical Conclusions, 111
Theoretical Perspective: a reappraisal, 115
Grass Roots Participation and Contemporary Politics, 128

Appendix: Theory, Methodology and Statistics 135

Bibliography 145

Index 151

List of Tables

2:1	Population and Housing Densities	35
2:2	Social Composition of Church Ward and Walton, by Socio-economic Groups (adult males)	39
3:1	Church Membership: Walton	50
3:2	Church Membership: Walton, Rank Correlation Comparisons	50
3:3	Attendance at Church Services: Walton	51
3:4	Attendance at Meetings of Associations: Walton	56
3:5	Past and Present Committee Memberships: Walton	56
3:6	Voluntary Association Participation: Walton	57
3:7	Voluntary Association Participation: Walton, Rank Correlation Comparisons	59
4:1	Socio-economic Groups: Walton	69
4:2	Voluntary Association Participation and Occupational Class: Walton, Rank Correlation Comparisons	71
4:3	Types of Schools Attended: Walton	73
4:4	Age on Leaving School: Walton	74
4:5	Home Tenure: Walton	77
4:6	Self-assigned Social Class: Walton	82
4:7	Self-assigned Social Class: Walton, Rank Correlation Comparisons	82
4:8	Scale of Radical/Conservative Attitudes: Walton, Rank Correlation Comparisons	85
4:9	Political Attitudes, Self-assigned Class and Occupational Class: Walton, Rank Correlation Comparisons	87
5:1	Self-designated Opinion Leadership: Walton	92
5:2	Self-designated Opinion Leadership: Walton, Rank Correlation Comparisons	92
5:3	Readership of Daily Newspapers: Walton	95
5:4	Numbers of Daily Newspapers Read: Walton	96
5:5	Number of Daily Newspapers Read: Walton, Rank Correlation Comparisons	97

10 List of Tables

5:6	Reported Interest in Newspaper, Radio and Television Topics: Walton, Rank Correlation Comparisons	100
5:7	Voluntary Association Activity and Interest in the Mass Media: Walton, Rank Correlation Comparisons	101
5:8	Scale of Authoritarian/Liberal Attitudes: Walton, Rank Correlation Comparisons	106
5:9	Scale of Authoritarian/Liberal Attitudes: Walton, Standardised Rank Correlation Comparisons	107

Preface

This monograph seeks to provide a contribution to the sociological understanding of political participation in contemporary society. This is a very broad question for a very short volume, and its treatment is necessarily selective and circumscribed. The main focus of attention is the theoretical significance of party membership, and the empirical material of the study is to be seen chiefly as a case study for illustrating the theoretical argument. I think such an approach may have more relevance to practical questions of political participation than a more detailed descriptive one, which is why this volume is not addressed solely to an academic audience. On the other hand, the approach adopted has resulted in the exclusion of anything more than a very superficial consideration of the workings of local party organisations: so the reader who is looking for a local study of constituency politics, or any kind of community study, will be disappointed.

The theoretical framework of the study is the theory of mass society. Sociologists and political scientists familiar with this theory may be aware of its influence and pervasiveness, and at the same time its somewhat unsystematic and value-loaded nature. Here the concern is solely with a small selection of the propositions of the theory, and these are to a large extent derived from Professor William Kornhauser's *Politics of Mass Society*. It should be made clear that the theory developed here utilises only certain aspects of Professor Kornhauser's work, leaving out aspects such as the role of *élites* and the details of his typology of societal types – communal, pluralist, mass and totalitarian. Furthermore, in developing the theory here, a number of departures have been taken from Professor Kornhauser – notably in the attempt to separate the theory from a consensus approach to political sociology. In this particular endeavour a considerable intellectual debt should be acknowledged to the work of Professor Ralf Dahrendorf. Whatever criticisms may be made of the theorists of the Mass Society, the author must bear sole responsibility for any failings of the theory as it stands here. An attempt has been made to remove ideological biases from the theory, and to present an objective analysis, but not by means of escape into the ephemeral ivory tower of value freedom. The value-orientation underlying this study, expressed in the titles of the book and the first chapter, is explicit throughout.

I am deeply grateful to Mr J. A. Banks for his invaluable guidance throughout the conduct of the research and for kindly reading and commenting on the manuscript. I am also much indebted to Mr Barry Hindess for many useful discussions while the research was in progress, and for his comments on the manuscript. I would like to thank Professor Richard Rose and Mr K. F. Dixon for kindly reading and commenting on the manuscript. I am indebted to the officials of the Liverpool Conservative, Labour and Liberal parties for their kind co-operation and assistance, and to several individual members of the departments of Social Science and of Political Theory and Institutions at the University of Liverpool for their interest and helpfulness.

This monograph incorporates much of the substance of a thesis approved for the award of the degree of Master of Arts by the University of Liverpool.

University of Strathclyde DAVID BERRY
December 1968

1 Political Participation and Democracy

Whether or not a society may be regarded as democratic depends in part on the extent and spread of participation by its members in the political process. Even if a high level of political participation is not in itself a sufficient condition of democracy, a society in which only a tiny minority of the population play any significant part in the political process could hardly be called democratic. Interest in political participation in Britain has tended to be focused on the one hand on electoral behaviour and on the other on the activities of very small groups, from local party leaders to professional politicians, more centrally involved in political activities. From this the impression may be gained that the only significant form of political participation for all but the very few engaged actively in political decision-making is voting, and that moreover this is a most satisfactory state of affairs. Even the fact that turnout is well below 100 per cent at general elections and usually below 50 per cent at local elections is a matter for congratulation, indicating the stability of democracy (Lipset, 1960: p. 32), and reflecting tolerance of the politically apathetic (Morris Jones, 1954). There are in fact good reasons for rejecting the notion of high electoral turnout as an indicator of the effectiveness of democracy. This suggests that voting in itself is perhaps not a very significant form of political participation. Voting in West Germany has been consistently high since 1945, but this does not prevent Dahrendorf from concluding that attachment to democratic institutions is weak: the 'unpolitical German' votes regularly, but is not really interested in politics (1968a: pp. 342-3).

In Britain there are other forms of political participation which involve sizeable minorities of the population. The claim of British political parties to be democratic rests not only on their electoral support and internal organisation, but also on their mass memberships, which are able to participate in and influence the decisions of the parties. At the constituency level the parties could hardly claim to be democratic mass organisations if they were composed solely of small bands of activists without any substantial body of rank-and-file members. As it is, according to a recent estimate (Richard Rose, 1965: p. 94) there are over three million individual party members in Britain. These have not attracted very much interest on the part of sociologists and political scientists; which may be because the majority of party members are apparently politically inactive, doing no more for their parties than paying their subscriptions, and most of the remainder are active only at election times. The view of McKitterick (1960) that Labour Party membership is dependent on recruiting campaigns and little else, and that party members are important only as election-campaign workers is certainly plausible, though, as I hope to demonstrate in this monograph, rather inadequate.

Given, then, that most party members are more or less inactive, membership in itself may nevertheless be regarded as a form of political participation. Apart from voting, it is the formal criterion of participation which includes the largest sector of the population, and it does, of course, involve considerably more than mere electoral support: a definite and open undertaking of support is made to the party, a form is signed, a subscription paid, and the member receives a party card. If party membership is seen as a form of political participation, and the spread of political participation as a key component of democracy, then the mass memberships of political parties surely contribute something more fundamental to the democratic process than labour for electoral machines.

In focusing on the significance of party membership for the workings of political democracy it follows that this study is not primarily concerned with differences in social composition and other similar factors between the membership of different political parties, but rather with the *common factors* of party membership, the nature and significance of party membership itself, irrespective of party. The emphasis on the differences between the parties in most British studies of party membership to date, such as those of Benney, Gray & Pear (1956: ch. 3) and Bealey, Blondel & McCann (1965: ch. 13) would seem to suggest that political participation as such is taken for granted and not in any way problematic, and that the only important question is why people participate in one party rather than another. Clearly differences between the parties are important in any study of political participation; the extent to which parties channel the interests of conflicting groups in society, and how far they are seen to be different by the populace, have important consequences for the workings of a democratic political system. Nevertheless the fact that under 10 per cent of the electorate are individual members of political parties in itself indicates that political participation other than voting cannot be taken for granted. The empirical evidence presented in this study thus consists more of comparisons between party members and samples of the electorate who are not members of political parties than of comparisons between the membership composition of different parties.

The widely acknowledged fact of the low level of direct political activity of the rank-and-file membership of political parties suggests that a study of them would not be very fruitful if it was to be restricted to an analysis of their roles within the parties, even if this was accompanied by the traditional analyses of age, sex, social class and religious affiliation. In a democratic society, however, political activity in terms of influencing and participating in decision-making processes is not restricted to political parties or formal political institutions. The importance of pressure groups in the British political system has long been recognised by both politicians and political scientists. The popular image of pressure groups is perhaps of very small groups of people influencing political decisions 'behind the scenes' in terms of their interests and out of all proportion to their numbers. This is not altogether an inaccurate picture, and indeed political scientists are usually more interested in the behaviour of the leadership of such pressure groups in their exercise of power than in the lower levels of political activity within pressure groups. Most pressure groups are in fact voluntary associations, or alliances of voluntary associations, which, like political parties, possess substantial numbers of rank-and-file members and are often organised in terms of local branches.

In a broad sense, rank-and-file membership and participation in voluntary associations may be seen as a further form of grass roots political participation. Most, if not all, voluntary associations may be regarded in some sense as interest groups, and as such as potential pressure groups: the rank-and-file membership of such organisations thus forms the basis of the political activity of such pressure groups. More specifically, participation in the activities of voluntary associations is political in so far as it involves participation and influence in decision-making processes. Moreover, most voluntary associations are formally, if not in practice, organised along democratic lines.

If democracy involves participation and influence in decision-making processes, then the extent to which a society is democratic depends on the degree of citizen participation in associations which are not overtly political as well as in explicitly political associations. Therefore, in taking party membership as a formal criterion of political participation there are good reasons for examining the extent to which party members participate in non-political voluntary associations: such participation may provide some indication of the importance of party membership in a democratic political system.

Except for the final chapter of this book, no further mention will be made of pressure groups as such, and our attention to non-party political bodies is restricted to voluntary association participation at the local level. Research and theory on voluntary associations has advanced much further in the United States of America, and indeed in other European countries, than in Britain, and it is this work rather than previous British research that forms the larger part of the empirical and theoretical basis of this study. The emphasis of American research on voluntary associations has tended to be on their contributions to social integration to the neglect of what is suggested by the notion of 'pressure group': namely, that voluntary associations, as conflicting, and possibly class-based, interest groups, are concerned with the exercise of power in society.

Theoretical Perspective

The theoretical framework to be outlined for this study derives more from developments in research on voluntary associations than that on political parties. As the concern here is chiefly with party membership, this does involve, in a sense, regarding party membership as a form of voluntary association participation. This may be considered justifiable in view of the marked similarity of previous research findings, referred to in the following chapters, for explicitly political participation and voluntary association participation. Evidence from a number of American and European studies indicates that political participation and participation in voluntary associations are closely related to each other, and that a number of factors, such as newspaper readership, opinion leadership, democratic and tolerant attitudes, and various indicators of social integration, are similarly related to each type of participation. However, this does not mean that party membership is regarded primarily as a form of social activity, but quite the reverse: our interest is not in the social consequences of political activity, but in the political consequences of social (voluntary association) activity. As suggested above, activity in both political parties and voluntary associations may be regarded as political participation in that it relates to participation and influence in decision-making in society.

This chapter began with the assertion that a society in which only a tiny minority play any significant part in the political process is not democratic: such a society, in which perhaps the centralised state is operated by a few individuals on the one hand whereas the atomised masses participate in politics only to the extent of choosing these individuals in elections on the other, may be called the mass society. In an urban industrial society the masses of the population are atomised in so far as they are deprived of the strong local community ties, the *Gemeinschaft* relationships of the pre-industrial *folk* society. Therefore industrial society requires the development of new links between the individual and his primary group on the one hand and the centralised state on the other to prevent the rise of the mass society. These new links take the form of secondary associations, based on work groups, neighbourhood and other interests; these secondary associations contribute to the social integration of individuals in industrial society, and the flourishing of such associations contributes to the maintenance of a pluralist democratic society.

This is the essence of what is now generally known as the theory of mass society, a theory which largely originated in the work of Alexis de Tocqueville. As Bell has suggested, 'Marxism apart, it is probably the most influential theory in the Western world to-day' (1960: p. 21). During the course of its development the theory has received contributions from a number of sociologists and social theorists, including several famous ones. It has fostered ideologies of both the left and the right, though mainly the latter, many of which are ably exposed by Bell (1960: ch. 1) and Bramson (1961). At the same time its theoretical sophistication for sociological analysis has advanced considerably, the most noted work of recent years being that of Kornhauser (1960), to which this study is considerably indebted.

The immediate relevance of the theory of mass society here is the postulate that participation in secondary associations, including political and non-political voluntary associations, is functional for the social integration and the maintenance of a pluralist democratic society. Before elaborating upon this basic postulate, for the benefit of those readers who may be sensitive to the use of such words, 'functional' does not here imply a functionalist theoretical approach, nor is 'integration' intended to be equated with either harmony or consensus; although in some of the American work referred to, notably that of Lane (1959), 'integration' appears to have such a meaning. Dahrendorf has drawn attention to the dangers of confusing social integration with social harmony: 'The confusion is dangerous because it suggests that creating harmony is the first task of politics; but this can never be accomplished except by repression. This confusion is erroneous because there may be well-integrated communities in which lively conflicts take place' (1968a: p. 195). For the purposes of this study, integration refers to the attachment of individuals to the political institutions, formal and otherwise, of society. Individuals are integrated in the polity in so far as they are identified with, or participate in, the activities of interest groups which are influential in the political process – the process of decision-making. That the conflicts between such interest groups may be intense emphasises the distinction between integration and harmony. Integrated individuals accept the existing political processes of society in so far as they are prepared to utilise such political processes for the expression of their interests either through participation in or identification with politically active groups which work through the existing political processes. Acceptance of institutionalised political procedures for articulating interests does not, however, necessarily involve agreement as to the ultimate legitimacy or moral value of such procedures. Integration does not, therefore, necessarily presuppose consensus.

It will be necessary at a later stage to examine in greater detail the relation between social integration and consensus, but with the basic distinctions outlined, attention may now be focused on the proposition that participation in political and non-political voluntary associations is functional for social integration in a pluralist democratic society. Arnold Rose (1954: ch. 3) has claimed that voluntary associations distribute power over social life among large sectors of the population, that they provide their participants with a sense of satisfaction with modern democratic processes, and also provide mechanisms for instituting social changes: they are 'modern democratic society's substitute for the integrated group of the primitive or folk society' (1967: p. 206). Rose's theory, as most of the work in the field, is specifically related to American society, but he does nevertheless consider that it might well be applicable to Britain and other European countries. Participation in voluntary associations, seen as political participation, is a form of participation and influence in decision-making processes, and as such clearly contributes to the distribution of power in society. A sense of satisfaction and understanding of democratic processes is provided in that the individual is able to participate in and observe such processes first-hand rather than viewing them as distant affairs of the state of little relevance to his everyday life. This is because, as mentioned above (p. 16), most

20 The Sociology of Grass Roots Politics

voluntary associations are formally democratic, though it might be observed that if in practice they deviate too far from the democratic norm, they may give rise to cynicism and dissatisfaction with 'democracy' on the part of those excluded from power and influence. The extent of democracy in practice, in terms of distribution of participation and influence in power, is always a matter of degree, and probably most voluntary organisations exhibit some tendencies towards Michels's famous 'Iron Law of Oligarchy'. The structure of organisations is not, however, the prime concern of this study. Whatever the practice of formally democratic associations, the very fact that they are formally democratic means that they possess democratic ideologies and in this they help to foster democratic norms and values. Voluntary associations operate as mechanisms for instituting social change in that they distribute power over a wide range of interest groups in society: changes may result from the conflicts of such interest groups in that the balance of power between conflicting interest groups is continually changing.

It must now be asked whether these functions of voluntary associations are dependent upon any special conditions over and above the possession of formally democratic constitutions. Here our approach may be explicitly distinguished from that of the functionalist school. A sound exposition of a functionalist theory of voluntary associations has recently been given by Smith (1966), who has proposed that voluntary associations are important for the maintenance of order in society in that they contribute to each of Parsons's four functional imperatives. His assertion that all types of voluntary associations are functional for the maintenance of all types of society would, however, seem to be of little heuristic value and perhaps little more than an exercise in taxonomy. The position taken here is that under certain conditions voluntary associations *may* be functional for the maintenance of democratic institutions in society. They are not seen as mechanisms of equilibrating processes in society after the analogy of homeostatis because, at least for the purposes of this study, the postulate of such processes is unnecessary. Finally the concern here is with the contributions of associations to democracy, not to order, social control and stability.

Having said this, the conditions under which voluntary associations contribute to social integration and democracy may now be considered. Voluntary associations are integrative and conducive to democracy if they broaden the range of social contacts of their members by introducing them to people with different interests and political views, and occupying different positions in the social structure. The broadening of social contacts is integrative, on the one hand, and, in that it broadens the political outlook of the individual in exposing him to opinions and interests which may differ from his own, is conducive to tolerant and non-authoritarian attitudes on the other. The importance of such attitudes for democracy lies in the assumption that people adhering to them are likely to be favourably disposed to the participation in the political process by people who do not agree with them.

Now, whether participation in voluntary associations does in fact result in broadening the social outlook of the members, rather than the mutual reinforcement of prejudices, again depends on a number of conditions. These conditions hang very much on the proposition that voluntary associations are *secondary* associations. Secondary associations are formed by groups of people who have particular common interests, and their shared interests are served by such associations. Yet each member, in addition to the interest he shares with other members of the association, possesses a whole range of other interests which are not so shared. Thus the association represents only one aspect of the member's life interests, and the control of the association over the member is only over a limited range of his conduct. The member's commitment to the association is partial and segmented – he has other commitments – and the control of the association over the member is partial and limited, rather than total. In such an association, if social interaction overflows the narrowly defined common interests, then the member will be exposed to other interests and opinions which he may not share. It is useful here to refer to the evidence from an American study by Curtis et al. (1967–8), showing that the development of friendships in secondary associations (clubs, neighbourhood and workplace) is associated with a marked decline in prejudice. Voluntary associations contribute to democratic processes in society in so far as they are voluntary secondary associations, that is in so far as the commitment they require from and the control they exercise over the individual are partial rather than total.

If partial commitment and control are the first conditions for the theory, they are by no means the only ones. These conditions result in the exposure of the member of a voluntary association to differing interests and opinions, but they do not guarantee it, as evidenced by a cricket club with a membership that is both politically and socially homogeneous. A further crucial condition for the theory, then, is that the membership of any one association should be heterogeneous rather than homogeneous in social composition.

As secondary associations are partial and limited in scope, focusing on narrowly defined interests, then it is quite likely that any one individual in a complex industrial society will belong to several such associations, including those of workplace and neighbourhood as well as voluntary associations. If membership of a voluntary association that is heterogeneous in social composition broadens the individual's social perspective, it follows that as the number of memberships held by any one individual increases, then so does the range of social contacts, opinions and interests to which he is exposed. Multiple membership of heterogeneous associations is thus of particular significance for social integration and democracy.

The question as to whether membership of a voluntary association is conducive to broadening the individual's perspective or to reinforcing his prejudices has been answered in terms of partial commitment and control, and social heterogeneity. Whether or not multiple memberships further broaden the individual's perspective depends on the extent to which his interests served in one association are not reinforced by participation in other associations: perspective is broadened only by multiple memberships which are pluralistic or cross-cutting in terms of interests, and not by memberships which are cumulative or superimposed along, for example, social class or religious lines. In fact, if voluntary associations in society are predominantly heterogeneous in social composition, it is likely that multiple memberships will be pluralistic and overlapping, though this is not necessarily the case. On the other hand, it logically follows that pluralistic multiple memberships are impossible if associations are characterised by homogeneous memberships: the heterogeneity of association memberships is thus a necessary, but not sufficient, condition for pluralistic patterns of multiple memberships. Furthermore, the partial commitment of and control over the members of associations are necessary, but not sufficient, conditions for both heterogeneous memberships and pluralistic multiple memberships. As Arnold Rose (1954: ch. 3 & 1967 ch. 7) and Kornhauser (1960: pp. 76–90) have argued, participation in voluntary associations under these conditions contributes to social integration and the maintenance of democracy in society. The strength of such secondary, intermediate group relations is, according to Kornhauser (1960: pp. 76–90) and Allardt (1962), crucial for the existence of a pluralist society, and their absence characterises the mass society.

The characteristics of voluntary associations discussed above, particularly in the case of multiple memberships, have consequences not only for social integration and democracy in terms of pluralities of loyalties conducive to democratic attitudes and the distribution of power and influence, but also for conflict and consensus. The reason for this is, as explained by Dahrendorf (1959: pp. 213–15), that the superimposition of interest groups in society acts to increase the intensity of societal conflicts, whereas the cross-cutting, or pluralism of interest groups acts to reduce the intensity of conflicts. Explicitly concerned with voluntary associations, Verba (1965) has hypothesised that pluralistic patterns of memberships in voluntary associations, resulting in cross-pressures of organisational influence, act in reducing cleavages in society, whereas superimposed memberships intensify cleavages. If pluralistic patterns of multiple memberships are thus conducive both to social integration on the one hand and the reduction of conflict on the other, it is not too difficult to see the plausibility of equating integration and democracy with harmony and consensus. As Lipset (1960: pp. 203-16) has argued, drawing on the evidence of several voting studies, cross-pressures of interests and influence result in moderation and reduction in intensity of political views, often accompanied by withdrawal of electoral participation. Cross-pressures thus contribute to the stability of democracy, and therefore an electoral turnout that is well below 100 per cent is a sign of a healthy democracy. However, when one adds the evidence of Milbrath (1965: p. 132) from a wide range of studies to the effect that cross-pressures inhibit and reduce political participation, and that participation is higher for people belonging to homogeneous groups than heterogeneous ones, something of a paradox appears. If the distribution of political participation is a key component of democracy, it may appear a little odd that mechanisms which contribute to political apathy are functional for the democratic process!

It is entirely consistent with the theory of mass society that cross-pressures should be conducive to moderation in political attitudes. As Shils (1956: part IV) has argued, democratic pluralist politics are the politics of moderation. The superimposition of interests is not conducive to democracy in so far as this gives rise to extremist politics, politics that are likely to be anti-democratic in so far as the superimposition results in the total isolation of the parties from each other and breakdown of communication channels between them. The mass society is, however, a society of atomised and largely politically apathetic individuals, and it would be inconsistent with it to suggest that if cross-pressures are conducive to apathy they are contributing to the maintenance of pluralist democracy. It must suffice here to point out that the evidence of Milbrath and Lipset is taken from voting studies, and that there is other evidence, shown by Himmelstrand (1962), that cross-pressures reduce electoral participation, but not political involvement.*

The conditions of voluntary associations that are conducive to democracy and social integration may be seen also as conducive to the reduction of the intensity of social conflicts. Intense

* The question of apathy is discussed at greater length in Chapter 6, pp. 120-6.

conflicts may endanger democracy in so far as they give rise to extremist anti-democratic political movements, but the danger lies in the fact that the interest groups are polarised and isolated from one another, and not from the existence of conflict *per se*. As Dahrendorf (1968b: pp. 147–50) has argued, liberal democratic politics are the politics of conflict.

American Theory and British Society: the relevance of class conflict

The theory of mass society as outlined here is primarily an American theory, and as such has been tailored very much for explanations of American society. American political parties are socially heterogeneous, drawing support from all major social segments, and as such give rise to cross-cutting solidarities (Kornhauser, 1960: p. 80), whereas, according to the popular view, British parties are class-based parties and as such are socially homogeneous. It might therefore follow that while the U.S.A. approximates the model of the pluralist democratic society, the theory is just not applicable to British politics, which are more appropriately seen in terms of class conflict. Such an argument, in my view, betrays both American parochialism and British insularity: there are, as I hope to show, good reasons for considering American politics to be more class-based than British politics!

Although American parties may not be class-based in the sense that any major political party claims to represent the interests of any particular social class, social class is an important variable in the sense that, irrespective of party, as disclosed by most of the American studies of political participation referred to in the following chapters, working-class people are less likely to participate in politics than middle-class people: political activity is largely a preserve of the middle class, and thus American politics might be regarded as class-based in that both the major political parties are largely middle-class parties. Furthermore, virtually all the American studies referred to on voluntary association participation, which we have regarded as a form of political participation, indicate that middle-class people are much more likely to participate than those of the working class. The implications of such findings have been noted by Arnold Rose and Hausknecht:

> the largest proportion of lowest income people in our society do not participate in voluntary associations and they therefore have little contact with persons of other classes and little power in the community as a whole. The lower income person is effectively, although not legally, segregated in his neighbourhood, his church, and possibly his labor union. (Rose, 1967: p. 246)

> Given the low rate of working class membership in associations, whatever functional consequences flow from association membership do not affect the working class. (Hausknecht, 1962: p. 122)

British studies of participation in voluntary associations have also indicated that such participation is predominantly middle class, and that such working-class participation as is found is largely segregated from middle-class participation. From the evidence of a local study, Bottomore (1954) has indicated that memberships are segregated very much in terms of occupational status, and that even in associations with memberships of mixed statuses there was little social intercourse between the different status groups: he also found that the leadership of associations was disproportionately middle class. In their study of Derby, Cauter & Downham (1954: pp. 71–2) also found strong social class differences between the membership of different types of associations: furthermore they found that middle-class people were more likely to join associations, and much more likely to be multiple members than the working class.

It is impossible to generalise from the evidence of two local studies both published as long ago as 1954, but although they seem to agree with American findings that voluntary association participation is predominantly middle class, there appears to be more emphasis on the segregation of social classes within associations, rather than the virtual exclusion of the working class. Turning to political parties the evidence is much more general and more conclusive: as shown by Benney et al. (1956:

pp. 47-8) and Bealey et al. (1965: p. 250) Labour Party members are overwhelmingly working class, and Conservatives middle class. Similar findings have led some sociologists to conclude that British politics are thus to be seen in terms of class conflict. It is useful here to refer to Stacey's study of Banbury (1959: pp. 51-4), suggesting that social cleavages are superimposed upon political cleavages along social-class lines resulting in the social isolation of the Labour Party. It is doubtful whether such a view of extreme polarisation of classes and the associated superimposition of social and political cleavages is of much general validity in Britain; Richard Rose's (1968) recent argument, to the effect that although class differences are very important in British politics, an explanation in terms of class determinism is inappropriate owing to the existence of a number of divisions in society which are along other than class lines, is probably more acceptable.

In fact, the extent to which political participation in Britain reflects social-class interests need not be considered in detail here, for the important point is that the close relationship between class and party means that political participation *per se*, in forms such as party membership, is not a predominantly middle-class activity. Because Labour members are overwhelmingly working class and Conservatives middle class, political participation overall is not markedly related to social class. If social-class interests are important in society, as many sociologists are at pains to make us believe, then the fact that such interests are channelled through participation in the political process may be seen as conducive to democracy. As a contributor to mass society theory, Arendt (1958: pp. 314-15) has stated, democratic politics are the politics of interest groups.

So far it has been observed that in America both party political participation and voluntary association participation tend to be largely middle class, whereas in Britain, apparently, only participation in voluntary associations is similarly related to social class. The relationship between political participation and voluntary association participation, reported in a number of studies discussed in Chapter 3 (pp. 53-4), might, in the case of America, be at least in part explicable in terms of social class:

the two forms of participation are related because they are both middle-class activities. However, if it is found that both sorts of participation are related in Britain, then this sort of explanation is clearly inadequate. There is, unfortunately, no comparable British evidence, but there is evidence from other European countries with party systems that are class-based in the same sense as the British system. Allardt & Pesonen (1960) have reported evidence of the relationship between political participation and membership of voluntary associations in Finland: elsewhere Allardt (1964) has suggested that Finnish politics are overwhelmingly class-based in terms of voting. Rokkan (1959) has shown evidence of a relationship between party membership and membership of other organisations in Norway: elsewhere Rokkan & Campbell (1960) have observed that Norwegian political parties are largely homogeneous in terms of social class. The significance of these findings is twofold: first of all, as political participation in Norway and Finland is not largely middle class, they suggest that the relationship between political participation and voluntary association participation is a very general phenomenon and not a function of social class, a point which has been made by Mayntz (1960). It might therefore be anticipated that similar findings are likely to apply in Britain. More important, if the relationship holds for working-class parties, it may be hypothesised that party systems which are class-based in terms of support are likely to result in the integration of the working classes in the political process not only through participation in the parties, but through participation in voluntary associations which is associated with participation in the parties.

To return to the rather controversial assertion made at the beginning of this section, American politics may be seen to be more class-based than British politics because the working class are, in a sense, more likely to be excluded from the political process in America than Britain. The relationship between social class and politics in Britain suggests not that the theory of mass society is inapplicable, but rather the reverse, that its application may be more fruitful in Britain in that it may be relevant to somewhat larger sections of the community. The immediate

Political Participation and Democracy 29

relevance of social class for the analysis in this study is the extent to which interest groupings, in this case multiple memberships of associations, are superimposed upon social-class lines.

Summary and Preview of the Empirical Study

The distribution of political participation in society has been regarded as a measure of democracy. This study is focused on the contribution of party membership as a formal criterion of participation to the maintenance of democracy: party membership may be seen as intermediate between minimal participation, voting, and the participation of the very small section of the population more centrally involved in decision-making processes in society. Grass roots participation in the activities of voluntary associations is to be seen as a similar form of intermediate participation, and because the evidence is that most party members are not very active in the parties, it is suggested that it may be useful to look at the relationship between party membership and participation in voluntary associations. It has been proposed that party membership might be examined in terms of the theory of mass society, which hypothesises that under certain conditions participation in voluntary associations is functional for social integration in a pluralist democratic society and inhibits the characteristics of the mass society. That the theory is largely American is not seen as a sign that it is more appropriate for the analysis of political participation in America than Britain, because the crystallisation of party support along social-class lines in Britain indicates that the working classes are more likely to be integrated in the political process than in America, where all forms of participation are disproportionately middle-class activities.

Thus our theoretical approach has been outlined in general terms. In the following four chapters the analysis moves away from national and even international generalisations to the empirical analysis of party membership in one constituency, and one ward of a different constituency, in the city of Liverpool. This analysis, of what is in fact a very small-scale empirical study, should be seen as a case study for examining the validity of the theoretical propositions put forward in this chapter, rather than a local community study in the usually accepted sense. The following chapter describes the empirical procedure of the study and gives an outline of the social characteristics of the communities where the study was carried out: local characteristics may have consequences for the relationships between variables which are theoretically important. In Chapter 3 the political participation of the party members is examined, both in terms of party activities and participation in other voluntary associations: the extent to which this participation is superimposed upon, or overlaps party political lines, is also considered. Chapter 4 is concerned with the extent to which the membership of the parties is homogeneous in terms of social class, and the degree to which multiple-association memberships are superimposed along social-class lines. Chapter 5 deals with the relationship between political participation and newspaper readership, opinion leadership, and authoritarian attitudes. As will be shown, all of these variables are directly relevant to our theoretical approach in terms of social integration.

The sixth and final chapter embodies the conclusions of the study and reassesses the theory of mass society in the light of the empirical findings and comparative evidence referred to. If the reader has found some questions unanswered and issues dismissed too briefly in this introductory chapter, I hope he will find at least some of the answers there. The chapter ends with a discussion of the relevance of the findings and theory to some of the practical problems of democracy in contemporary British society. It is my view that the practical application of sociology to social problems is likely to proceed more from theory developed in conjunction with empirical research than from the publication of huge quantities of empirical data, and I submit this as a justification for the rather broad theoretical emphasis in this otherwise rather limited empirical study.

2 The Approach to Empirical Analysis: Procedure and Community Structure

The empirical study presented in this book derives from the evidence obtained through interviews with random samples of the membership of the Conservative and Labour parties, and a random sample of the electorate, in the Walton constituency of Liverpool. This survey was preceded by a somewhat smaller pilot survey of the membership of the Liberal Party and again a sample of the electorate in a single ward, Church ward, of the Wavertree constituency of Liverpool, and evidence from this pilot survey is also utilised. The task of this chapter is twofold: firstly it is to set out the empirical procedure of the study: the broad theoretical framework provided in the introductory chapter does not in itself delineate operational procedures. Secondly the purpose here is to give an indication of the significant social characteristics of the two areas studied: the Walton constituency and Church ward of Wavertree constituency. It will be seen that the comparison of the findings for these two areas is particularly interesting in that there are marked social differences between the two areas: as mentioned above (p. 30), and as is made more explicit below (pp. 34–5), local neighbourhood characteristics may have consequences for the determinants of political participation.

Procedure

Our selection of party membership as the formal criterion of political participation for this study is one that would appear to involve few problems of operational definition. As indirect membership is excluded, notably that of party membership by virtue of trade union membership, party members are those who individually subscribe to a political party, hold a membership card, and presumably have their names recorded on membership lists. In practice the position is not quite so clear. It is widely accepted that party membership lists are often to a greater or lesser extent inaccurate: furthermore the parties are not monolithic organisations based on ward or constituency parties. Apart from the trade union sections of the Labour Party, all three parties considered here possess numbers of associated or subsidiary organisations, such as youth sections, women's sections and political clubs. Membership of the last-mentioned group may or may not require card-holding party membership.

The sample of Liberal Party members was selected from a list of people who either helped the party in the ward or were members of one of the subsidiary organisations – the Young Liberals or the Women's Liberal Association. The list is thus not quite the same as a list of formal party members, but, although the ward party was well organised, this was the only list available. For practical purposes, however, the list may be considered the equivalent of a membership list.

The sample of Labour Party members was selected from the membership list of the Walton Constituency Labour Party, with the exclusion of those who were not recorded as having paid their subscriptions during the previous twelve months. The Labour Party list was particularly convenient in that it both recorded all the individual members in the constituency and indicated whether subscriptions had been paid.

The sample of Conservative members was selected from the membership lists of the ward parties and Young Conservative branches of the Walton Conservative Association. These were not the only lists available of the Walton Conservative Association, but no names were taken from the three others – those of members of political clubs, trade union group leaders and members of the ladies' sections. Members of Conservative clubs, unlike those of Labour clubs, are not required to be party members: the trade union group leaders were listed under the ward parties if they were party members. The ladies' sections were excluded for no other reason than that women already considerably outnumbered men in the ward parties. There are thus slight differences in the criteria for selection of the members of the Conservative and Labour parties, but these are largely

The Approach to Empirical Analysis 33

dictated by the differences in the party organisations, and in each case the criteria may be considered to give perhaps the best fit with the formal criterion of party membership.

In order to provide a check against any inaccuracies in the party lists, those members selected for interview were interviewed only if they answered in the affirmative an initial question as to whether they were paid-up members of a political party. This resulted in the exclusion of 17 per cent of the Labour sample and 18 per cent of the Conservative sample. The same question was put to those people comprising the sample of non-members selected from the electoral roll, though in Walton this resulted in the exclusion of only two people who were party members.

All the samples were selected at random by the use of random numbers, and in Walton all three samples were stratified by polling district to ensure a proportionate spread of the samples throughout the constituency. Members under the age of 21 years were excluded from the Liberal Party sample, as this age group would not be represented in the sample of the electorate. In Walton this age group was not excluded from the sampling frame of the party membership lists, but in the analysis of the data these persons are taken into account only for comparisons between the Conservative and Labour parties, and are excluded from comparisons between party members and the electorate. In Walton 56 Labour members, 54 Conservatives and 61 electors were interviewed. The original samples were very much larger, but most of the drop-out was a result either of excluding people from the survey after they had answered the initial question as to whether they were party members, or of people moving away. The response rates for each sample, calculated as the percentage of people interviewed out of those suitable for interview, were 80 per cent for the Labour sample, 83 per cent for the Conservative sample, and 78 per cent for the electors. In Church ward 29 Liberal Party members and 25 electors were interviewed. The interviews in Church ward were conducted during February and March 1965, and those in Walton between October 1965 and February 1966 inclusively.

No explanation has been given here of the empirical methodology of the study: the reader will find an explanation of the rank correlation statistics employed in the analysis, and a discussion of other methodological issues, in the Appendix.

Walton Constituency and Church Ward

Although it would hardly be conventional not to give some description of the areas studied, such description is of some theoretical consequence here, for it shows that, in very broad terms, Church ward may be seen as a middle-class area and the constituency of Walton as a working-class area. It should, however, at the outset, be admitted that the circumstances through which this comparison is possible are purely fortuitous. The areas were chosen partly for convenience and partly through the desirability of selecting local parties which were well organised and thus likely to have reliable lists for sampling purposes. It was again fortuitous that Walton should have been recommended by the officials of both the Labour and Conservative parties.

Before giving a description of the areas studied, it is useful to indicate in what way community characteristics affect social and political participation. First of all there is considerable American evidence to show that as size of community (Hausknecht, 1962: p. 18) and level of urbanisation of the community (Greer, 1958) increases, then the level of participation in voluntary associations declines. This may indicate a weakness of the theory of mass society, which posits that voluntary associations are functionally more important in large urbanised communities, because it is in these that local community ties are weakest and where, consequently, social relations are most likely to be atomised. Rather than comment on this here, it will simply be noted that both areas for this study form parts of an English city with a population of approximately three-quarters of a million people. Most of the other relevant evidence focuses on the relationship between socio-economic neighbourhood characteristics and social and political participation. A study of San Francisco has shown that family and economic neighbourhood characteristics influence the development of informal group relations between friends, relatives, neighbours and co-workers

The Approach to Empirical Analysis 35

(Bell & Boat, 1956–7), and that participation in voluntary associations is higher in high status areas independent of the social status of the individuals concerned (Bell & Force, 1956). In Britain there is evidence that neighbourhood factors are significant intervening variables between socio-economic class and voting. This is suggested by Bealey et al. (1965: p. 185) in their study of Newcastle under Lyme, and more clearly demonstrated in a study of class voting in local elections in Liverpool. In this, Hindess (1967a and 1967b) has indicated that because the relationship between social class and voting in any one neighbourhood depends upon the social-class composition of the neighbourhood, there is no clear or consistent relationship between class and voting for the city as a whole.

There appear to be good reasons for concentrating on broad socio-economic factors, and this will be done in terms of characteristics of housing and occupational-class composition of the areas.

Table 2:1 Population and Housing Densities

	Persons per acre	*Persons per room*	*% of persons at density above 1·5 persons per room*
Liverpool	26·8	0·73	11·7
Church ward	23·3	0·54	3·2
Walton			
Inner wards: County	45·3	0·65	5·7
Warbreck	30·6	0·63	4·1
Outer wards: Fazakerley	21·6	0·68	6·9
Pirrie	19·6	0·77	9·9

SOURCE: 1961 Census, Lancashire County Report.

Density of population is perhaps a useful overall indicator of degree of urbanisation, and does, in the first column of Table 2:1, show marked differences between the two inner wards of Walton, those nearest the city centre, and the more peripheral wards. County ward is nearest to the city centre and in places bordering on the central residential districts of the city. At the time of the study the predominant housing in this ward was terraces of small unimproved nineteenth-century cottages, built at very high densities. County ward also includes part of a large low-density inter-war housing estate, and although the ward has a much higher population density than the others studied, and one well above the average for Liverpool, it is still well below the densest ward of the city, populated by 104·9 persons per acre. The houses of Warbreck ward are also mainly of pre-1914 construction, though they are generally of a much better quality and built at lower densities than those of County ward. In Pirrie ward, apart from a pocket of privately built inter-war housing, the pattern is uniformly one of municipal housing. Most of this is low-density inter-war development, but there is also a sizeable recently completed development which is of high density and contains a high proportion of multi-storey flats. It should be added that the low density of persons per acre in Pirrie ward is partly a function of the considerable amount of both open space and land taken up by non-residential developments in the ward. This is also very much the case for Fazakerley ward, though here the housing is somewhat more diversified, containing fair amounts of inter-war private housing, Victorian terraced properties of varying quality, and a municipal housing development under construction at the time of the study, as well as a large area of inter-war municipal housing.

Although there are thus considerable variations between the four wards comprising the constituency of Walton, they are all very different from Church ward. Although this ward is somewhat nearer to the city centre than either of the outer wards in Walton, its population density is not much higher than that for these Walton wards: moreover, unlike the case in the outer Walton wards, Church ward is almost entirely residential. The housing in Church ward is also much more diversified than in any of the Walton wards, ranging from substantial detached properties of the 1930s, which are some of the best houses in the city, to small unimproved nineteenth-century terraced housing and large Victorian houses converted into flats, which are in some case substandard and little different from the accommodation of the inner rooming-house districts of the city. The ward should not, however, be seen as providing a contrast of poverty and affluence, for most of the housing falls between these extremes: most of it consists either of the better type of pre-1914 terraced housing or the characteristic private semi-detached developments of the 1930s.

The indices of persons per room and percentage of persons living at a density of more than 1·5 persons per room are probably the more useful measures of urban structure, and provide a clear indication of the differences between the Walton wards and Church ward. Directly they provide some indication of overcrowding, but it is useful here to draw attention to an analysis of census data for Merseyside and Hampshire by Gittus (1963–4), showing that persons per room is a high predictor of other indices of urban structure. The difference between Walton and Church ward in terms of persons per room is very substantial when the range of this measure within all the wards in Liverpool, from 0·53 to 1·11 persons per room, is considered. Although all the Walton wards, with the exception of Pirrie, are below the city average, Church ward in fact has the second lowest density of all the wards in the city. The measure of overcrowding in the third column of Table 2:1 is very much a reflection of the figures for persons per room, and again the figure is lowest for Church ward. The range within Walton, although perhaps appearing high, should be compared with the range for all the wards of the city, which is from 1·1 per cent to 38·1 per cent of persons living at a density of more than 1·5 persons per room.

In general terms the evidence indicates that average housing standards are considerably higher in Church ward than in Walton, though those in Walton, close to the average for the city as a whole, are far above those of the worst parts of the city. Turning now to the evidence of the occupational-class composition of the areas studied, similar differences are apparent.

The index of occupational class employed here is that of the Registrar General's classification of socio-economic groups.*
As this index is employed throughout this study as a measure of

---

* These are fully described in the Registrar General's *Classification of Occupations* (H.M.S.O., 1960).

social class, it is worth while here to set out the necessary details. There are, in fact, 17 socio-economic groups, but these may be classified into six categories as follows:

1. Groups 3 and 4: professional workers.
2. Groups 1, 2 and 13: employers and managers.
3. Groups 8, 9, 12 and 14: skilled and own-account workers.
4. Groups 5 and 6: non-manual workers.
5. Groups 7, 10 and 15: personal service, semi-skilled and agricultural workers.
6. Groups 11, 16 and 17: unskilled workers, H.M. Forces, and those not elsewhere classified.

For some of the analysis presented in this study, a sixfold classification is too complex; but by combining categories 1, 2 and 4 (socio-economic groups 1–6 and 13) and categories 3, 5 and 6 (socio-economic groups 7–12 and 14–17) a dichotomy emerges which approximates the distinction between manual and non-manual occupations. Runciman (1966: pp. 43–52) has used this distinction in his major study of social stratification in Britain. He has produced evidence to suggest that this is the basic stratification dividing line in British society, and has proceeded by regarding the terms 'working class' and 'middle class' as broadly synonymous with the manual and non-manual strata. Similarly, here the three categories grouped as non-manual occupations – professional workers, employers, managers and other non-manual occupations will be regarded as middle class and the three manual categories as working class. It should be emphasised that this is only an approximation, and one not without anomalies, but this is the case for any classificatory scheme. It will simply be noted here that fortunately none of the people interviewed were or had husbands who were officers or enlisted men in H.M. Forces. Further discussion of indices of social stratification is reserved for Chapter 4.

Using this index of occupational class, marked differences appear in the social composition of Church ward and Walton. The largest differences occur in the first two and last two categories: the proportion of professional workers, employers and

Table 2:2 Social Composition of Church Ward and Walton, by Socio-economic Groups (Adult males)

	Church ward %	Walton constituency %
(1) Groups 3 & 4	6·5	1·4
(2) Groups 1, 2 & 13	15·3	6·3
(4) Groups 5 & 6	25·2	18·9
Non-manual groups	46·9	26·6
(3) Groups 8, 9, 12 & 14	35·2	39·3
(5) Groups 7, 10 & 15	10·0	18·0
(6) Groups 11, 16 & 17	8·0	16·1
Manual groups	53·1	73·4

SOURCE: 1961 Census, 10% sample.*

managers living in Church ward is almost three times larger than that for Walton, whereas the proportion of semi-skilled and unskilled workers, represented approximately by categories 5 and 6, in Church ward is not much above half that for Walton. Taking the manual/non-manual distinction, there is little difference in the proportions for each of these groups in Church ward, whereas in Walton the proportion in the manual group is nearly three-quarters. It is suggested that this evidence, taken together with the evidence on housing, indicates that Church ward may be characterised as a middle-class area and Walton as largely a working-class area. If our characterisation of Church ward appears a little surprising in that manual workers are still in the majority there, it should be considered that these people are in fact in the majority almost everywhere, and most certainly in almost any ward of a large city such as Liverpool. The notion of 'middle-class area' here refers to an area in which the proportion of middle-class residents is well above average but not necessarily equal to or above that of working-class residents.

It would hardly be appropriate to conclude this description of the local communities without some mention of their patterns

* The census data are not published in a form to allow analysis by ward of constituency, and I am grateful to Barry Hindess for providing the data from which this table was computed.

of voting in elections. The constituency of Wavertree, in which Church ward is situated, returned a Conservative M.P. with a majority of over 5000 over the Labour candidate in the 1966 General Election. At the time of the study the ward was represented by one Liberal and two Conservative councillors in the city council, and at local elections during the time of the study Labour candidates ran a very poor third to Conservative and Liberal candidates. Walton, a Conservative seat in the 1959 General Election, was a Labour gain in 1964, and in 1966 returned the Labour M.P. with a majority above 5000 over the Conservative candidate in a straight fight. At the time of the study there was no organised Liberal Party in Walton. The voting patterns of the two areas may be seen to bear some correspondence to their social characteristics.

At the beginning of this section evidence was referred to showing that the social composition of a neighbourhood may exert an independent influence on the direction of political participation and the extent of participation in voluntary associations. Such comparisons cannot be undertaken here because of the modest scale of the study, and especially the very small sample sizes for Church ward. However, in so far as the correlates of participation appear similar for both areas the case for generalisation is strengthened in that these correlates appear to apply in both middle-class and working-class areas. In fact, as is shown in the following chapters, there are indeed strong similarities: there are also marked differences, as in the case of the relationship between home ownership and participation, which permit some inferences as to the way in which the social composition of a neighbourhood may affect the determinants of participation.

3 Political Activity and Social Participation

The generally accepted fact that most party members are more or less inactive in their parties does not mean that a study of party membership can afford to ignore party political activity and deal solely with the relationship of various 'social' factors to party membership, but rather that a somewhat broader view should be taken of political participation. In the introductory section of Chapter 1 the case was advanced for considering membership and participation in the activities of voluntary associations as a form of political participation in that it relates the members and participants to decision-making processes in society. Therefore specifically party political activity is only one aspect, albeit the most important one, of political participation for party members; and membership and participation in the activities of voluntary associations represents another. The first section of this chapter examines party political activity: factors considered are attendance at ward meetings and meetings of other party organisations, committee memberships, membership and participation in the activities of political clubs, and helping the parties at election times. In this section, confined to the evidence from the study of the Conservative and Labour parties in Walton, the focus is very much on the differences between the two parties which, as will be seen, are considerable.

The following sections examine the relationship between party membership and participation in voluntary associations, drawing on the study of Liberal Party members in Church ward, as well as that of party members in Walton, and also on the samples of people from the electorate of the two areas. Here the emphasis is on the difference between party members and non-members, although differences between the parties which are important are taken into account: trade union membership, associated very much with the Labour Party, is dealt with separately, as is church membership and attendance, owing to the strong association on Merseyside between party affiliation and adherence to particular religious denominations. Participation in all other types of voluntary association is not distinguished by any further categorisation, but treated together. The description of the relationship between party membership and voluntary association participation is then followed by an examination of the relationship between party activity and voluntary association participation; that is, whether or not the more active party members are likely also to be more active in other associations. Finally some consideration is given to the extent to which participation in other associations is superimposed along party lines: how far Labour Party members are found in one type of association and Conservatives in another. The theory of mass society hypothesises that only multiple memberships which are pluralistic or overlapping, rather than superimposed, are conducive to social integration and democracy, and the implications of the findings for the theory are noted.

Party Activities

A number of previous British studies have indicated not only that most party members are inactive, but also that Labour Party members are more likely to be active than Conservative members. Blondel (1963: pp. 93–4) has suggested that something like two-fifths of Labour members, and between one-third and one-quarter of Conservative members are at least minimally active. That Labour Party members are the more active is explicable, it is suggested, in the larger individual membership of the Conservative Party, thus including more lukewarm supporters than that of the Labour Party. Turning to local studies, Birch (1959: ch. 5) has reported Labour Party members to be more active than Conservatives in Glossop: in Greenwich, Benney et al. (1956: p. 49) found that higher proportions of Labour members than Conservatives held party offices, attended meetings and helped the party, and that Labour members appeared to be more interested in politics than Conservatives. In their study of Newcastle under Lyme, Bealey et al. (1965: p. 265) found that three-quarters of the Labour members helped at elections compared with just under two-fifths of the Conservatives. That even for the Labour Party members the general level of activity is very low is indicated by the evidence of Donnison & Plowman (1954): in what they considered to be one of the most active wards in Manchester (Gorton South ward) they found active Labour Party members to be in a very small minority: only 11 per cent had attended a ward meeting in the past month, and only 19 per cent in the past six months.

Much of the evidence referred to points in the same direction, and it may therefore appear a little surprising that the evidence from Walton should be inconsistent with it. For almost every level of political participation measured, activity was much higher among Conservative members than among the Labour members. Taking first attendance at ward meetings, the figures for attendance at a meeting during the month prior to interview are so low as to prevent any realistic comparisons: only four Labour members (7 per cent) and six Conservatives (11 per cent) reported attendance. However, taking what may be considered to be the minimal criterion of political activity, help at election times, exactly half the Conservative members reported helping at election times in comparison with just a quarter of the Labour members. Another marked difference between the parties was the high level of membership of and participation within subsidiary party organisations within the Conservative sample, in contrast to a total absence in the Labour sample of similar membership and participation: twenty-two (41 per cent) of the Conservatives were members of either a women's branch or a Young Conservative branch, and seventeen Conservatives (31 per cent) had attended a meeting of one of these subsidiary organisations during the month prior to interview.

The difference in participation in subsidiary party organisations is perhaps in part related to the much higher proportion of women in the Conservative sample, and consequently a larger potential membership for the Conservative women's branches: thirty-three (61 per cent) of the Conservatives were women, compared with nineteen (34 per cent) of the Labour members. It may here be noted that several previous studies, including those of Bottomore (1954), Benney et al. (1956: p. 47) and Bealey et al. (1965: p. 255) have found the proportions of women to be much higher in the Conservative Party than in the Labour Party. More important, however, in explaining the differences in participation between the parties is the much greater emphasis within the Conservative Party on social, as opposed to more strictly political, activities.

Within the Walton Conservative Association there were, at the time of the study, no fewer than six women's branches – one each in Pirrie and County wards, and two each in Warbreck and Fazakerley wards. Each branch holds a weekly or fortnightly meeting in one of the Conservative clubs in the constituency, with the exception of the Pirrie branch, which meets on other premises, and these meetings are as much social as political occasions. There were, at the time of the study, four Young Conservative branches in Walton, one for each ward, and these again meet weekly or fortnightly. No detailed study has been made of the activities of these branches, but it is useful here to refer to a paper by Abrams and Little (1965), which suggests that three-fifths of the activities of Young Conservatives, by far the largest youth movement attached to a political party in Britain, are social rather than political: the movement is to be seen as a political movement only in so far as it provides a recruiting ground for party workers. In Walton it would appear that for both the Young Conservatives and the women's branches the provision and attraction of social activities does contribute to the level of specifically political activity of members of the Conservative Party: once people have become involved in social activities, they are more easily recruited for work during election campaigns. The Labour Party in Walton is much more narrowly political in focus, and much less concerned with social activities. At the time of the survey there was a women's section attached to the constituency Labour Party with a small active membership meeting monthly: there was also a Young Socialist organisation, though this was also small and not very active. As has been mentioned above, none of the Labour Party members interviewed acknowledged membership of these organisations.

The more developed social activities, particularly within the

Political Activity and Social Participation 45

subsidiary organisations, of the Conservative Party in Walton, is probably a major factor involved in another large difference between the parties. Only one Labour member interviewed served on a committee of the party or a party organisation, whereas no fewer than sixteen (30 per cent) of the Conservatives interviewed were members of some committee of the party or a party organisation. Even if a number of these were on committees or sub-committees of a purely social rather than political nature, the difference between the parties is no less striking, the more so when it is considered that seven of the Conservative committee members sat on more than one committee. Five of the Conservative committee members were members of ward or divisional executive committees, and the one Labour committee member was an officer of the constituency executive committee. It is probably these people, with the addition of a Conservative Party member who was a city councillor, but not on one of these committees, who represent the core of political activists. It should be noted here that a small-scale study of the rank-and-file party membership is unlikely to include a significant section of such activists, and because of the smallness of their numbers it would be unwise to generalise about the incidence of such activists within the constituency parties. Random samples are not necessarily representative samples, and it may be that the Conservative sample contains one or two above the proportionate number of 'core' political activists, and the Labour sample one or two below the proportionate figure. However, taking committee memberships as a whole, there can be no doubt that the incidence of participation in committees is much higher in the Conservative Party than in the Labour Party in Walton.

An account of the participation of the party members within their parties would not be complete without some discussion of the role of the political clubs. For both parties these are primarily social organisations, but in that nearly all party meetings take place in the clubs, an active club member is very likely to come into contact with the political activities of the parties. In the Walton constituency there are three Labour clubs and four Conservative clubs. There is little difference in the proportions from the two parties reporting membership of a club and attendance at a club during the month before the interview: 57 per cent of the Conservatives and 54 per cent of the Labour members reported club membership, and 13 per cent of the Conservatives and 12½ per cent of the Labour members reported club attendance. Although the figures for attendance are very much smaller than those for membership, they might indicate the proportion of stalwart club members, as most of them visited their clubs weekly if not more frequently. These figures may, however, conceal some differences in the relative importance of the clubs of each party, because the Labour clubs require their members to belong to the Labour Party, whereas the Conservative clubs, in addition to party members who belong, have a large membership of people who are not members of the Conservative Party. One important difference to emerge from the survey relates to the membership of committees of the political clubs: eight (15 per cent) of the Conservatives, but no Labour members were on club committees. This difference may reflect a more developed range of social activities in the Conservative clubs, and it may be added that five of those eight Conservative club committee members also sat on other party committees. That the political clubs are important recruiting grounds for party members, though more so for the Conservative Party than the Labour Party, is suggested by the facts that eighteen (33 per cent) of the Conservative members and twelve (21 per cent) Labour members said they joined at least in part through the social attraction of the clubs.

It has been argued that the higher level of participation found in the Conservative Party is explicable at least in part in terms of the greater emphasis on social activities within the Conservative Party. On the one hand, much of the participation is social rather than purely political, and, on the other, once people are involved in social activities they can more easily be persuaded to do some political work. There is other evidence for regarding the Conservative Party members as more socially and less politically orientated than those of the Labour Party. In explaining how they came to join the party, considerably fewer Conservatives (17 per cent) than Labour members (30 per cent) mentioned party policies or political principles, which would

Political Activity and Social Participation 47

seem to be consistent with the findings of Benney et al. (1956: p. 49) that Labour members were more interested in politics than Conservatives. The most frequent replies to the question as to how they came to join were in terms of the influence of family, relatives, husbands and wives, and friends, but they were more prominent in the Conservative sample (63 per cent) than among Labour members (46 per cent). Finally the greater incidence of replies in terms of the social attractions of the political clubs among the Conservative members has already been noted.

In concluding this section, some further comment would seem to be called for on the inconsistency of the findings reported here with those of the studies referred to all showing Labour Party members to be more active than Conservatives. Blondel (1963: p. 94) suggested that the Conservative Party membership tended to be larger as a result of recruiting drives and thus contains a higher proportion of lukewarm supporters. In Walton, however, there was little difference in the size of membership between the parties, each party possessing approximately 1000 members. Canvassing and recruiting drives, in contradiction to McKitterick's (1960) claim, did not anyway appear to be an important source of recruitment, as only four Labour members and three Conservatives mentioned them in explaining how they came to join the party. Further to these comments, it can only be suggested that as previous evidence is confined to very few local studies, the case for generalisation is limited and the discovery of contradictory evidence in one constituency is therefore not unduly surprising. As the present study is considerably more recent than those referred to, the possibility exists that a decline in activity has taken place in the Labour Party, but clearly no such inference can be made from the evidence of a single local study.

Trade Union and Church Memberships

These may appear as a somewhat odd combination, but, as explained in the introduction to this chapter, they do possess a common factor in that they are both forms of activity which are likely to vary according to political affiliation. Trade union memberships and church memberships were not considered apart from memberships of other voluntary associations in the study of Church ward, and so the evidence is again restricted to Walton.

Dealing first with trade union membership, the evidence confirms a strong relationship between Labour Party membership and trade union membership. 55 per cent of the Labour members, compared with 15 per cent of the Conservatives and 23 per cent of the comparative sample from the electorate, were members of trade unions or professional associations. The proportion of trade union members in the category of electors is much closer to that for the Conservative group than for the Labour group, but in making this comparison two factors should be taken into account. Firstly, of the eight Conservatives belonging to trade unions or professional associations, only five belonged to trade unions in the accepted sense, the other three belonging to professional associations. If this suggests an emphasis on the low level of trade union membership among the Conservatives, another important factor to be considered is that the social composition of the Conservative sample would render few of the Conservative members eligible for trade union membership. As mentioned in the previous section, the majority of the Conservatives were women, and the majority of Labour members men: the proportions of the sexes were, as would be expected, much more even in the sample of the electorate, though here men were slightly in the majority. Apart from the sex differences between the samples, the occupational-class composition, as described in the next chapter, is such that proportionately far fewer Conservatives than people from the other samples are eligible for trade union membership by virtue of their occupations. In all, the evidence cannot then be taken to indicate that the Conservatives are less likely to join trade unions than the non-party members: conclusive evidence exists only for the strong relationship between Labour Party membership and trade union membership, and it is worthwhile adding here that nine of the Labour members (16 per cent) said they joined the party through trade union activities.

Turning now from trade union membership to church

Political Activity and Social Participation 49

membership and attendance, it is first necessary to draw attention to the traditional association between support for the Labour Party and affiliation to the Roman Catholic Church, and support for the Conservative Party and affiliation to the Church of England, which is very marked in Liverpool. This suggests that religious differences among party members are likely to be superimposed upon party divisions, but before considering the evidence, something must be said about the operational definition of church membership as this is not quite so clear-cut as trade union membership. The interest here is not in religious identification, religious involvement and religiosity as such, but in membership and participation in specific religious organisations. In a recent paper, Goode (1968) has suggested that religiosity and religious involvement differ in kind from formal church participation, and that the latter may be seen as a form of voluntary association participation. The people interviewed were therefore not asked to state their religion, but instead they were asked if they belonged to any particular local church, and to give the name of the church as well as the denomination. To counteract the possibility of the number of people reporting church membership being inflated through people not wishing to admit that they did not belong to a church, the question was included as a sub-section of the more general question as to whether they belonged to any local organisations. In considering the evidence, church membership has been categorised by denomination, but it should be emphasised that this is not evidence of religious affiliation as such, and the high proportion of people who are not church members in each sample cannot be assumed to be either more or less 'religious' than the church members.

From the figures in Table 3:1, it is immediately apparent that the vast majority of Labour church members are Roman Catholic, and an even larger majority of the Conservative church members Church of England. There is, then, considerable evidence that religious differences are superimposed upon party divisions, but a comparison between all three samples is necessary to put this evidence in its proper perspective. Although the proportion of Church of England members is much higher

50 The Sociology of Grass Roots Politics

in the Conservative sample than in the sample of electors, and similarly the proportion of Roman Catholics in the Conservative sample much lower, there are proportionately no fewer Church of England members among the Labour members than

Table 3:1 Church Membership: Walton

	Lab.	Cons.	Electors
Church members			
Church of England	4	22	5
Roman Catholic	16	4	10
Other churches	4	4	2
	24	30	17
Not members of churches	32	24	44
	56	54	61

Table 3:2 Church Membership: Walton
Rank Correlation Comparisons*: Church members: non-members

	Values for γ	Values for γ with proportions of sexes standardised
Conservatives: electors	0·550	0·521
Labour: electors	0·334	0·361
Conservatives: Labour	0·250	0·197
Party members: electors	0·443	0·444

among the electors. Furthermore there are more members of other churches in both parties than in the sample of the electorate, though here the numbers are too small to be of any real significance. Comparison of all three groups suggests that the

* In this and other tables of correlation coefficients, the values refer to the probability that members of the first-named group are more likely to possess the attribute (in this case church membership) or to be ranked higher in terms of the attribute than the other group. The comparisons between the party members and electors are not directly calculable from Table 3:1 as party members under the age of 21, included in Table 3:1, are excluded in these comparisons. The operational interpretation and method of computation of the statistic γ and method of standardisation are explained in the methodological appendix.

Political Activity and Social Participation 51

superimposition of religious differences upon party divisions is relative and far from absolute, in that there is a measure of overlap between the two parties and the different religious denominations.

The interest here in the superimposition of church and party allegiance should not lead us to overlook a somewhat different aspect of the evidence. If denominational differences are ignored, then it is apparent from Table 3:1, and more explicitly demonstrated in Table 3:2, that party members are more likely to belong to a local church than the electors. Of the three groups it is the Conservatives who are most likely to belong to churches, and although the probability is somewhat less for Labour members, the pattern for these is closer to the Conservatives than the electors. Some of the difference between the two groups of party members is in fact accounted for by the differences in the proportions of men and women between them. It is widely accepted, as shown in Bottomore's local study (1954), that women are in the majority in religious organisations, and in Walton it was found that with the three groups combined the probability that women were more likely to be church members than men was expressed by the coefficient $\gamma = 0.310$. If church membership is seen as a form of voluntary association membership, then the evidence here would appear consistent with the evidence from previous studies referred to in the next section showing a relationship between party membership and voluntary association membership.

Table 3:3 **Attendance at Church Services: Walton**
Rank Correlation Comparisons: Labour:electors, $\gamma = 0.114$.
Conservative:electors, $\gamma = 0.280$.

	Lab.	Cons.	Electors
At least weekly	16	11	12
At least monthly	1	14	5
Less than monthly	39	29	44
	56	54	61

The pattern for church attendance, shown in Table 3:3, is similar to that for church membership, though here the differences between the groups are very much smaller. The differences between the groups in terms of weekly attendance and attendance less than weekly but at least monthly would appear to be partly a function of the proportion of Roman Catholics in each group: it is probably not very surprising to find that members of Roman Catholic churches are more likely to attend church weekly than Anglicans. No distinction has been made between those reporting attendance less frequently than monthly and those who never attended, as it is likely that a number of people may have said they went to church occasionally because they did not like to admit they never went to church.

There are no exactly comparable findings from previous British research as the relationship between party membership and religion has usually been examined in terms of simple religious identification or affiliation. The findings here are not necessarily contradictory to those of Benney et al. (1956: p. 47) and Bealey et al. (1965: p. 257), who found Labour Party members more likely to have 'no religion' than the general population of the constituencies studied, because evidence of church membership and attendance is not evidence of religiosity as such.

Trade union and church memberships have been considered together in this section because they are both voluntary association memberships which are likely to be superimposed upon party divisions, and the evidence has shown this to be the case. That they are otherwise very different forms of social participation is obvious, but it is as well to make explicit the point that although church participation may be seen as a form of voluntary association participation, this is perhaps different in kind from other forms. Even if it is not an indicator of religiosity, attendance at religious services is clearly a very different kind of activity from attending meetings of voluntary associations. There is some American evidence, such as the local studies of Zimmer & Hawley (1959–60) and Goode (1968) and the analysis of national samples by Hausknecht (1962: p. 68), of an association between church attendance and voluntary association participation. However, in Britain, Stark (1964) has produced evidence from national samples showing that church attendance is not related to participation in other organisations. This may well be the case, as there is evidence from a study comparing new estates in Britain and the U.S.A. showing that American churches are much more active as social organisations than their British counterparts (Bracey, 1964: ch. 10). The evidence from Walton is that although overall church membership and attendance is not related to participation in other voluntary associations, among Labour members there was a negative relationship between church membership ($\gamma = 0.277$) and attendance ($\gamma = 0.327$) and voluntary association participation:* among the Conservatives, on the other hand, there was a positive relationship between church membership ($\gamma = 0.306$) and attendance ($\gamma = 0.289$) and voluntary association participation. These differences would seem to be explicable in that most Labour church members are Catholics, and most Conservative church members Anglicans. There is some American evidence (Hausknecht, 1962: pp. 52–3) to show that Catholics are less likely to belong to associations than Protestants.

Although there are grounds for considering church membership and attendance as somewhat different in kind from other voluntary association activities, this is not the case for participation in church or church-affiliated organisations. Consequently, membership, committee membership and attendance at meetings of these organisations are considered together with participation in other voluntary associations.

Voluntary Association Activities

There is a considerable body of previous research indicating a positive relationship between political participation and participation in non-political voluntary associations. Dahl (1961: pp. 298–9) has reported the positive association of political participation with participation in other organisations in New Haven, U.S.A., Erbe (1964), studying three Iowa communities in the

* For this analysis a comparison was made between voluntary association activists and people who were not activists in each sample. 'Association activists' are operationally defined on p. 58, below.

U.S.A., has found political participation to be positively related to involvement in other organisations, the relationship remaining high with a number of other factors controlled. From the evidence of a survey in Finland, Allardt & Pesonen (1960) have reported the positive association of political participation with membership of two or more voluntary associations. In a Norwegian study, Rokkan (1959) has reported that members of political parties had a higher number of memberships in other organisations than non-members, and that, furthermore, party members were more likely to have been decision-makers in these other organisations. A study by Hartenstein and Liepelt (1962) has indicated that party members in West Germany are more likely than non-members to participate in non-political activities, although the general level of party membership there is very low. In a study of the membership of the Italian Socialist Party, Barnes (1967: p. 122) has reported that those members who have high levels of participation in the party are more likely to belong to other voluntary associations. The American secondary analyses of Lane (1959: p. 166) and Milbrath (1965: p. 17) have both drawn attention to the relationship between political participation and social participation. From a study of the U.S.A. and four European countries, including Britain, Verba (1965) has reported that members of voluntary associations are more likely to be politically active than non-members. Finally, in an extensive secondary analysis of voluntary association participation in the U.S.A., Hausknecht (1962: pp. 49–51) has noted that voluntary association members were more likely to identify with a political party than non-members. The wealth of evidence showing the relationship between political participation and voluntary association participation is supplemented by findings that members of voluntary associations are more likely to be interested in and informed about politics than non-members. These are reported by Almond & Verba (1963: ch.11) in their study of the U.S.A. and four European countries, and noted by Lipset (1960: p. 196) from a survey of West Germany.

In this study the relationship between party membership and voluntary association participation is examined along three dimensions – those of membership, attendance at meetings and committee membership. Dealing first with membership, the evidence from Church ward was that over two-thirds of the Liberals in comparison with less than half the sample of the electorate were members of at least one formally organised voluntary association, including churches and trade unions. However, in Walton, with memberships of churches and trade unions excluded, little difference in the pattern of association memberships emerged between the samples. 36 per cent of the Labour members, 41 per cent of the Conservatives and 38 per cent of the electors belonged to at least one association.* A rank correlation comparison between the party members and electors, taking into account the proportions in each group with one, two and three or more memberships, produces the coefficient $\gamma = 0\cdot030$, indicating that there is virtually no difference between party members and electors.

The figures in Tables 3:4 and 3:5 for attendance at meetings and committee memberships include participation in trade union activities: at these levels of participation the figures are too small to permit separate analysis for the trade unions. It should also be pointed out that as the concern here is with comparisons between party members and non-members rather than inter-party comparisons, party members under the age of 21 are excluded from the analysis. Table 3:4 shows the numbers of people who have attended meetings of any associations other than party political ones during the month prior to interview. Although non-attenders are in a large majority in each group, the criterion of attendance employed is fairly exacting, and the figures might be taken as an indication of the incidence of regular attendance. Even if the attenders are in a small minority in each group, the incidence of attendance is much higher among the party members than among the electors, as indicated by the correlation coefficient.

The incidence of committee memberships is of more direct relevance to the study than either memberships or attendance at meetings, because this may be taken as a direct indicator of participation in the decision-making processes of voluntary

* More detailed figures for these association memberships are published in a paper by the author elsewhere (1969).

56 The Sociology of Grass Roots Politics

Table 3:4 Attendance at Meetings of Associations: Walton
Party members:electors, $\gamma = 0.358$

No. of meetings	Lab.	Cons.	Electors
Three or more	7	6	2
Two	2	3	5
One	5	3	1
None	41	37	53
	55	49	61

associations. Partly because committee posts are often held for limited periods of time, the evidence here refers both to posts held at the time of study and those held at any time previously. A further reason for considering past committee posts was that a fair proportion of the people interviewed might have given up committee work through reasons of age and health: one-third of the people interviewed in Walton were over 60 years old, the proportions being slightly above this in the Conservative sample and slightly below in the Labour group. The figures in Table 3:5 disclose a strong relationship between party membership and committee membership: the proportion of committee members among party members is three times as large as that among the electors.

Table 3:5 Past and Present Committee Memberships: Walton
Party members:electors, $\gamma = 0.574$

No. of committee posts	Lab.	Cons.	Electors
Two or more	9	5	3
One	11	11	4
None	35	33	54
	55	49	61

However, the differences between the categories of party members and electors in terms of attendance and committee membership do not obscure the fact that in each group the large majority do not participate at each level. Apart from its theoretical significance, this does mean that the correlation coefficients given, because they ignore the ties between the

Political Activity and Social Participation 57

samples at any one level of participation, somewhat overemphasise the differences. It is therefore useful to combine the evidence for memberships, attendance at meetings and committee posts in one table. If these three dimensions are seen as reflecting successively higher levels of participation, then by subdividing each level according to whether the activity is in one or more than one association, with a further category for past association memberships and the residual category of people who have never

Table 3:6 Voluntary Association Participation: Walton
Party members:electors, $\gamma = 0.314$

Level of activity	Lab.	Cons.	Electors
1. Committee members and/or attenders at meetings	23	20	11
2. Past or present members, not attenders	19	14	29
3. Not active	13	15	21
	55	49	61

joined associations, we have a table of eight levels of participation. Because of its complexity, this table is not reproduced here,* but the correlation coefficient computed from it, $\gamma = 0.287$, showing the probability that party members participate at higher levels than non-members is interesting. This correlation summarises the differences between party members and electors for every form of participation in voluntary associations apart from party political activities and church membership and attendance: although the value is somewhat smaller than those for attendance at meetings and committee membership, this is to be expected with a much more sensitive measure taking into account eight levels of participation instead of three or four. In Table 3:6 the eight levels of participation are collapsed into three categories. From this it is apparent that whereas the proportion of passive members of associations is somewhat higher among the category of electors, the proportion of people who are past or present committee members or attenders of associations is much higher among the party members. The

* This may be found as Table VIII of chapter 8 in my M.A. thesis (1967).

incidence of participation is fractionally higher for Labour members than Conservatives, but the difference here is so small as to amply justify the procedure of combining the two categories of party members for comparisons with the electors.

So that the analysis of the relationship between party membership and a number of social factors, presented in Chapters 4 and 5, should take into account the incidence of voluntary association activity, a simple distinction between voluntary association activists and non-activists is employed. Association activists are defined as those people who are past or present committee members or who have attended at least one meeting of an association during the month prior to interview. The numbers of such people in each group in Walton are shown in the first category of participation in Table 3:6. They are in a minority in each sample, but just over 40 per cent of the party members, compared with 18 per cent of the electors, are classified as association activists. It is interesting to note that in Church ward the proportions of party members and electors who were classified as association activists were almost exactly the same as those in Walton: 38 per cent of the Liberals and 20 per cent of the electors there were so classified.* It may be added that these differences in both Walton and Church ward are at an acceptable level of statistical significance.

One advantage from combining the two categories of party members in Walton for analysis is that the excessive proportions of men and women respectively in the Labour and Conservative groups cancel each other out. This is quite important as a number of previous studies have reported differences in the incidence of participation between men and women, and these differences appear to be much more marked in Britain than in America. The American studies of Hausknecht (1962: p. 31) and Agger & Ostrom (1956) have reported little difference in

---

* As the percentages for Church ward take into account only current, and not previously held, committee posts the incidence of participation would appear to be in fact somewhat higher than in Walton. This is to be expected as Church ward is a middle-class area. In further discussions it should be noted that 'association activists' in Church ward do not necessarily include people who have previously held committee posts.

participation between the sexes, though Scott (1957) found men had more memberships than women, but women attended meetings more frequently than men. The cross-national study of Almond & Verba (1963: p. 303) gives evidence of membership in associations for women being substantially lower in Britain than in the U.S.A. In Britain, Bottomore (1954) found that men predominated in all associations except those he classified as cultural or religious, and Cauter & Downham (1954: p. 64) found membership of associations much higher for men than women.

Table 3:7 Voluntary Association Participation: Walton Rank Correlation Comparisons

	Values for γ	Values for γ with proportions of sexes standardised
Conservatives: electors	0·516	0·613
Labour: electors	0·534	0·439
Conservatives: Labour	−0·028	0·237
Party members: electors	0·524	0·533

In Walton, with the three groups combined, it was found men were much more likely to be association activists than women, as described by the coefficient $\gamma = 0·674$. It is therefore not surprising that the standardisation in Table 3:7 has the effect of increasing the difference between the Conservatives and electors and reducing the difference between the Labour members and electors. The overall difference between party members and electors, however, remains virtually unchanged.

The analysis of the relationship between party membership and voluntary association activities is completed by the consideration of whether the more active party members are also more likely to be active in other voluntary associations. If the evidence presented in this section so far is of theoretical significance, then we would expect this to be the case; otherwise the relationship between party membership and activities in other associations might be explained in that people who are active in some voluntary associations are 'joiners', and as such are

60 The Sociology of Grass Roots Politics

likely to join a number of others, including political parties, in which they will be inactive. This explanation would be consistent with the rather plausible notion that as the amount of leisure time people have is limited, activity in one association means restricting activity in others. However, previous research would indicate that this is just not so. The most useful evidence to refer to here is that of Allardt et al. (1958) showing, from a national survey of Finnish young people, that a number of different forms of leisure activities are positively related to each other: officers of associations were found to belong to more associations than rank-and-file members. The authors have advanced the thesis, which is independent of but not inconsistent with the theoretical approach employed here, that leisure activities are cumulative and that successful participation in one sphere leads to participation in others.

For the analysis here, three levels of party activity are taken into account, namely, those who are on party or political club committees or have attended meetings, those who only help the party at elections, and those who are not active. Comparing the proportions of Walton party members who are voluntary association activists for each level of party activity, then the coefficient $\gamma = 0.292$ shows that the higher the level of party activity, the more likely are party members to be active in other voluntary associations. Among the party members, 53 per cent of the association activists, in comparison with 39 per cent of the non-activists, are at least minimally active for their party, and 35 per cent of the association activists are party committee members or attenders as opposed to 19 per cent of the non-activists. It may be noted that the relationship between party activity and activity in other associations is somewhat stronger among the Conservatives than among the Labour sample, which may be because many of the Conservative Party activities are more of a social nature and less narrowly party political. The relationship does, nevertheless, hold for both parties, and is directly comparable with the evidence of Barnes (1967: p. 122) that the more active members of the Italian Socialist Party were more likely to belong to other voluntary associations.

Party Divisions and Social Participation

This chapter began with an assessment of the party political activities of party members, and has proceeded with the examination of the levels of participation of party members in the activities of trade unions, churches and other voluntary associations. In the preceding section it has been shown that party members are more active in other associations than non-members, and that the level of activity in other associations tends to be higher for the more active party members. This concluding section returns to a question raised in our discussion of trade union and church memberships, namely as to how far membership and participation in voluntary associations tends to be superimposed along the lines of party political divisions. As stated in Chapter 1 (p. 22), it is multiple memberships of associations rather than single memberships which are of particular significance for the theory of mass society, and whether such multiple memberships are conducive to social integration in a pluralist democratic society depends in part on the extent to which they are cross-cutting in terms of interests rather than superimposed. Superimposition of interest groupings results in the isolation of interest groups from one another, and a narrowing, rather than the broadening, of people's perspectives which are conducive to tolerant and democratic attitudes.

Party members who belong to other associations are, by definition, multiple members of associations. It has been shown in this chapter that trade union and church memberships are largely superimposed along party lines, though in each case there is a measure of overlap: there are trade unionists and Roman Catholics in the Conservative group and there are a few Anglicans in the Labour group. A more detailed examination of this overlap discloses that both groups of party members each included at least one member from no fewer than five local churches – two Anglican, two Catholic and one Baptist – and three trade unions; each party group also had one officer from one of these trade unions. Detailed analysis of the extent to which memberships of other associations are superimposed along party lines in Walton is rather limited, because memberships of sixty-nine associations were reported from a total sample less than three times this size, and only seven of these mustered more than one member from the three sub-samples together. However, for two of these seven, an ex-service and a masonic association, memberships were reported by at least one member from each of the Labour and Conservative groups. A view of the general pattern of multiple memberships discloses that six Labour members, but no Conservatives, were members of works sports and social clubs, and that eight Conservatives, but only one Labour member, belonged to other social clubs. These differences are more likely to reflect occupational and more especially sex differences between the samples than party divisions, and apart from these there was little difference in the incidence of membership of different types of organisations between the parties.

Although the evidence of cross-cutting memberships among other associations is very limited, evidence of superimposition would appear to be confined to the churches and trade unions. It was stated in Chapter 1 (p. 23) that the superimposition of multiple memberships may be conducive to the enhancement of cleavage and conflict in society, and pluralism of memberships to the reduction of conflict or consensus. If the question here was whether the relative evidence of superimposition and pluralism merited a conclusion in terms of conflict or consensus, then I think the answer would have to be in terms of conflict: more memberships are superimposed than overlapping. However, this is not the important question here, as consensus, integration and democracy are not synonymous. The issue here is whether the superimposition of memberships along party lines is sufficient to indicate the social isolation of the two parties from each other, and this is surely not the case: the evidence of cross-cutting ties may be taken as sufficient to indicate the possibility of interlocking channels of communication, and it is only to be expected that small samples will produce very little direct evidence of this.

These remarks must remain somewhat inconclusive because factors of social class have not so far been taken into account:

the whole question is begged as to whether multiple memberships should be seen as superimposed along the lines of class as well as party, which in turn requires analysis of how far the membership of each party is homogeneous in terms of class. The next chapter attempts to answer these questions.

4 Party Divisions and Social Class

The importance of social class for the theory of mass society is nowhere more apparent than in the notion that the mass society is a classless society, and it is this notion that is the basis of the critique of Marxism in terms of the theory of mass society: the classless society is not the promised land following the Communist revolution and the dictatorship of the proletariat, but a society in which individuals are alienated, atomised, isolated and manipulated. As Arendt (1958: pp. 314–16) has suggested, democratic political parties represent interests in society and, as interests disappear, then so do politics of the democratic sort: if the class system breaks down, so does the democratic party system, because parties as interest parties can no longer represent class interests. Kornhauser (1960: pp. 47–9) has suggested that mass movements, which may be seen as miniature mass societies and are likely to develop into totalitarian movements, are classless.

It will be obvious that these arguments raise a number of rather complex issues not the least of which is the ideological appeal of mass society theory to Conservatives for its apparent justification of class inequalities. Here the concern is solely to explain how factors of social class impinge upon the analysis of party membership. Following Arendt, if class interests are important in society, then the channelling of these interests through participation in the political process is conducive to democracy: if the Labour and Conservative parties represent different class interests, then this means there are avenues for different social classes to participate in politics. In terms of the theory of mass society, however, pluralist democratic politics are not pure class politics: pure class politics means the complete superimposition of class interests upon party divisions, homogeneous class parties, and the resulting isolation from one another of classes and parties: as explained in Chapter 1, in terms of the theory of mass society, such politics are not conducive to social integration and democracy. This leads to the empirical questions as to how far the parties are heterogeneous in terms of social class and how far multiple memberships of party members are superimposed upon class divisions.

Before turning to the analysis of these empirical questions, it is necessary to spell out more specifically what is meant by social class in this context, as there is little consensus of opinion among sociologists on this. Lenski (1966: pp. 74–5) has suggested that class is a multi-dimensional term, because there are types of classes and class systems, and for the employment of the term in its widest sense this is reasonably uncontroversial. The procedure adopted here is to assume that there are different criteria for class divisions in modern society, and, as is explained below, these different criteria are relevant to the analysis in slightly different ways. Dahrendorf's (1959: pp. 74–7) distinction between social class and social stratification is also relevant here. He defines social class in terms of participation or exclusion from the exercise of authority in society: classes are seen as conflicting interest groups, and economic classes are a special case of the more general phenomenon of social class. Social stratification, on the other hand, refers to 'layers in a hierarchical system of strata differentiated by gradual distinctions': gradations of social status, income, education and style of life are gradations of stratification. Lenski's notion of power class as a type of social class is similar to Dahrendorf's concept of class: both recognise that there are several bases for social class defined in terms of power, though it must be added that their analyses are based on very different premises.

Using Dahrendorf's terminology, both social class and social stratification are relevant to the analysis here. The postulate that associations represent interests, and the question of how far these interests are cross-cutting or superimposed, are both central to the theory of mass society. In this chapter the concern with classes as conflicting interest groups is restricted to economic interests, though these may be regarded as only one aspect of social class in Dahrendorf's sense. Yet associations may be superimposed in terms other than those of social or power classes. As different status groups in society are distinguished by, among other things, different styles of life, one

Party Divisions and Social Class 67

factor distinguishing different life styles may be different patterns of participation in associations. Some voluntary associations, particularly those which restrict membership by social criteria, are instrumental in conferring social status upon their members: obvious examples are certain London 'gentlemen's clubs' and some English golf, tennis and cricket clubs. It may be mentioned that Gordon & Babchuk (1959) have proposed a typology of voluntary associations, one criterion of which is whether or not associations confer status or prestige on their members. It should be clear that if different status groups have their own associations and never mix with other status groups in different associations, the isolation of status groups from one another has similar consequences in terms of the theory of mass society to the superimposition and isolation from one another of interest groups in society. The distinction made here between social classes as power classes and status groups bears some resemblance to Max Weber's distinction between class and status, particularly as the interest in class here focuses on economic class: Weber also noted that parties, which in this context are interchangeable with associations, may represent classes or status groups.

It is a sad fact of sociological research that theoretical sophistication in the treatment of social class is not matched by similar refinements in empirical analysis, and in a modest monograph primarily concerned with other matters it is not the place to suggest remedies to this problem. The theoretical distinction between classes as conflicting interest groups and strata as a hierarchy of status groups becomes blurred in empirical analysis. The chief index of social class employed here, the Registrar General's Socio-Economic Grading (1960), is really a measure of occupational stratification which takes into account both economic and social status criteria. Other indices of stratification and class examined in this chapter are educational attainment, housing standards and home tenure, all of which partly reflect social status and partly more economic criteria of class.

The analysis begins with a consideration of the composition of the parties in terms of occupational class, and the relationship between occupational class and participation in voluntary association activities. The social composition of the parties is described further in terms of educational background, housing standards and home tenure. The relationship of home tenure to participation in voluntary association activities is also assessed. Finally, certain attitudes which are relevant to class and party divisions are analysed: evidence is presented of social-class identification, a scale of politico-economic radical/conservative attitudes, and the relationship between these variables and occupational class.

Occupational Class

The measure of socio-economic grading as an indicator of occupational class has already been employed in Chapter 2 to describe the social composition of the two areas of Liverpool studied, and on the basis of this and other evidence it was suggested that Church ward and Walton could be characterised as middle-class and working-class areas respectively. The classification employed here is close to that for the census data given in Table 2:2 (p. 39); married women and widows were classified according to their husbands' occupations as for the census data, but people who were not assignable to any category on the basis of occupation were excluded from the analysis instead of being included in category 6. For convenience, the list of categories is repeated here:

1. Groups 3 and 4: professional workers.
2. Groups 1, 2 and 13: employers and managers.
3. Groups 8, 9, 12 and 14: skilled and own-account workers.
4. Groups 5 and 6: non-manual workers.
5. Groups 7, 10 and 15: personal service, semi-skilled and agricultural workers.
6. Groups 11, 16 & 17: unskilled workers, H.M. Forces, and those not elsewhere classified.

Table 4:1 discloses that there are large differences between the parties in Walton, and that these are in the expected direction: the largest category in the Labour group is that of skilled manual workers, whereas in the Conservative group the largest category is that of employers and managers. The composition of the sample of the electors is close to that of the 10 per cent census sample of Walton, given in Table 2:2, and that the composition of the Labour group is much closer than the Conservative group to the electors is to be expected in a predominantly working-class area. Both groups from Church ward were predominantly middle class in that non-manual categories were in a majority in each group, though the proportion classified as non-manual was considerably higher for the Liberals than the electors.

Table 4:1 Socio-economic Groups: Walton
Rank Correlation Comparisons: Conservatives:Labour, $\gamma = 0.586$. Conservatives:electors, $\gamma = 0.507$. Labour:electors, $\gamma = 0.130$

Groups	Lab.	Cons.	Electors
1. 3 & 4	0	0	1
2. 1, 2 & 13	3	21	6
4. 5 & 6	11	11	12
Non-manual groups	14	32	19
3. 8, 9, 12 & 14	26	11	27
5. 7, 10 & 15	11	7	11
6. 11, 16 & 17	5	0	3
Manual groups	42	18	41
	56	50	60

The theoretical importance of the class composition of the sample is in terms of whether the parties are to be seen as heterogeneous or homogeneous in social composition, and large class differences between the parties do not necessarily mean that the parties are homogeneous class parties. In fact, in view of the spread of socio-economic groups among both categories of party members shown in Table 4:1, the Labour and Conservative parties studied would both appear to be fairly heterogeneous in social composition. The Liberal group from Church ward, more strongly middle class than the Conservative sample, could also be regarded as heterogeneous in that it

70 The Sociology of Grass Roots Politics

included people from all except the sixth category of socio-economic groups.

The evidence of the relationship between occupational class and participation in voluntary associations, to which attention is now turned, is most interesting, if only because it is not obviously predictable. Previous British and American research, as mentioned in Chapter 1, has indicated that middle-class people are more likely than working-class people to participate in the activities of voluntary associations. However, because the Labour Party sample is predominantly working class, but characterised by levels of voluntary association participation as high as those for the Conservative sample, one might not expect these findings to be repeated here. The alternative model, also mentioned in Chapter 1, of working-class people joining one sort of association and middle-class people a different sort, would seem initially to be more appropriate. If this is valid, and if participation in associations is superimposed upon party divisions along social-class lines, it would follow that the participation of Labour members is primarily in working-class associations, and that of Conservatives in middle-class associations. Consequently one would expect that among Conservatives middle-class members would be more likely than working-class members to be association activists, but among the Labour sample one would expect more working-class than middle-class members to be association activists.

Somewhat surprisingly, the evidence from Walton is not at all consistent with this alternative model. First of all, if all samples are combined, then the evidence is that people classified as non-manual are more likely to be association activists than people with manual occupations, as expressed by the coefficient $\gamma = 0.274$. The relationship is not particularly large, but it is consistent with previous research findings. More detailed analysis reveals that in fact this relationship is quite substantial for the categories of Labour members ($\gamma = 0.553$) and electors ($\gamma = 0.440$), but among the Conservative group a higher proportion of those people classified as manual than those who were non-manual were association activists, shown by the coefficient $\gamma = 0.250$. The evidence that middle-class Labour members

Party Divisions and Social Class 71

and working-class Conservatives are more likely to be association activists is not consistent with the thesis that multiple memberships which are superimposed upon party divisions are also superimposed along social-class lines.

Table 4:2 Voluntary Association Participation and Occupational Class: Walton
Rank Correlation Comparisons

	Values for γ	Values for γ with proportions of manual and non-manual groups standardised
Labour: electors	0·534	0·597
Conservatives: electors	0·516	0·582
Labour: Conservatives	0·028	0·024
Party members: electors	0·524	0·589

Because social class is related to association activities in different ways in each party group, the consequence of standardisation by social class is to increase the difference in levels of activity between each party group and the group of electors, as indicated in Table 4:2. This table also shows clearly that the factor of occupational class does not in any way account for the relationship between party membership and voluntary association activity.

The evidence for the relationship between occupational class and church membership is very similar, except that the differences between the groups are larger in this case. As for voluntary association participation, previous British (Stark, 1964) and American (Goode, 1968) evidence may be referred to indicating that middle-class people are more likely to participate in church activities than working-class people. In Walton, while this was found to be so among the Labour members ($\gamma = 0·351$) and markedly so for the electors ($\gamma = 0·576$), among the Conservatives it was the people classified as manual who were more likely to be church members, as shown by the coefficient $\gamma = 0·545$. That it is middle-class Labour members and working-class

72 The Sociology of Grass Roots Politics

Conservatives who are more likely to be church members would suggest that religious divisions which are superimposed upon party divisions are not necessarily also superimposed upon social-class divisions. It is worth adding here that eight of the twelve manual Conservative church members were Anglicans, and it might therefore well be the case that the superimposition of religious divisions upon party divisions is more significant in Walton than the superimposition of class upon party divisions; in view of the limitations of the evidence, however, this must remain a speculation.

In this section it has been argued that in spite of large differences between the parties, they may be regarded as reasonably heterogeneous in terms of occupational class. Occupational class has also been shown to be a significant intervening variable between party membership and both church membership and other association activities, but the evidence is such as to suggest that the superimposition of church memberships and other voluntary association participation upon party divisions is not matched by further superimposition upon occupational-class divisions. This evidence is fairly unambiguous, but is nevertheless very limited. In the first place no direct evidence has been given of the extent to which voluntary association participation and church membership are superimposed upon occupational-class divisions: the scale of the study is too small to permit analysis of the relationship between occupational class and such participation. Secondly this discussion has ignored one form of participation considered in Chapter 3, namely trade union memberships, which are determined by occupation and therefore quite obviously superimposed upon occupational class. Finally occupational class is only one limited index of social class and stratification: the evidence of lack of simultaneous superimposition of association participation and church memberships upon class and party cannot be conclusive because it may be that the index of occupational class does not distinguish the most significant class and status divisions in society. However, even with these reservations, the evidence of heterogeneity of party memberships and pluralism of multiple memberships is still very interesting. To return to a point made in the concluding paragraphs of Chapter 3, even if the evidence of cross-cutting ties is not sufficient for the conclusion that the pattern of multiple memberships is conducive to consensus rather than conflict, the case that this does indicate social integration rather than isolation in terms of the theory of mass society is strengthened.

Education and Housing

The description of the social composition of the membership of the different parties is broadened by considering the factors of education and housing standards. Dealing first with education, it might be expected that the differences between the groups in occupational class would also be reflected in differences of educational backgrounds. Two indices of educational background have been employed, and the first of these is a classification of type of school attended. The threefold classification

Table 4:3 Types of Schools Attended: Walton

	Lab.	Cons.	Electors
1. Independent or grammar school	2	11	8
2. Technical or central school	2	6	7
3. Secondary modern or elementary school	52	37	46
	56	54	61

employed here broadly corresponds to the three types of education provided for under the 1944 Education Act, three types which were supposed to be equal, but which in fact have been generally accepted as reflecting a hierarchy in terms of educational standards. Here independent schools have been grouped together with grammar schools, and central schools, pre-war institutions, with technical schools. In terms of this classification Table 4:3 reveals some considerable differences between each of the three groups which are in the same direction as the occupational-class differences, but in each group the vast majority were educated at secondary modern or elementary schools. It may also be noted that, in contrast to the findings for occupational class, of the two parties it is the Conservatives who are closer in educational background to the sample of electors. The educational background of both groups from Church ward emphasises the social-class differences between Walton and Church: the proportion of electors there who had attended secondary modern or elementary schools was just over two-thirds, similar to that for the Conservatives in Walton, whereas less than half of the Liberal Party members attended this type of school.

Table 4:4 Age on Leaving School: Walton
Rank Correlation Comparisons: Conservatives:Labour, $\gamma = 0.700$. Labour:electors, $\gamma = 0.596$. Conservatives:electors, $\gamma = 0.100$

	Lab.	Cons.	Electors
16 years or over	2	14*	7
15 years	5	9	11
Not over 15 years	49	31	43
	56	54	61

The other index of educational background employed here is that of age on leaving school, and for this some comparative evidence is available from previous British studies. The studies of Greenwich (Benney et al., 1956: p. 47) and Newcastle under Lyme (Bealey et al. 1965: p. 256) have both reported that whereas the majority of Labour members left school at the age of 14 years or under, the school-leaving age for most Conservatives was 15 or over: in each case the differences between the parties were very large. As shown in Table 4:4 the differences between the parties in Walton are in the same direction, but the proportions in each group are very dissimilar from those found in these earlier studies. The figures are very close to those for type of school attended: as shown by the correlation coefficients, it is again the Conservative group which is closer to the group of

* This figure includes all five Conservative members under the age of 21.

electors. More important, it is again the case that the overwhelming majority in each group are concentrated in the third category. For the Labour group the school-leaving-age distribution is close to that reported in the Newcastle and Greenwich studies, but the Conservatives are very different, with a much higher proportion receiving only the minimal length of schooling. In considering this evidence it should be borne in mind that, depending on their age, people interviewed may have been at school when the minimum legal school-leaving age was 13, 14 or 15 years.

In the discussion of occupational class it was concluded that in spite of very large differences between the parties, they could be seen as fairly heterogeneous in social composition. The picture is somewhat modified by the evidence on educational background: in that for each index most members of both the Conservative and Labour parties are found in the minimal category, the differences between the parties in terms of these indices are small. It might be said that both parties are fairly homogeneous in terms of educational background, but as this is the same for both parties, this homogeneity is of no theoretical consequence here: educational background is no basis for party divisions. This homogeneity does render any analysis of the relationship between education and participation in voluntary associations impossible, because there are too few people in the higher categories. Although in Church ward it was found that participation in voluntary associations was positively related to education as measured by type of school last attended, in Walton, however, it may be assumed that the small size of the educational differences between the samples means that education may be discounted as a factor in explaining the level of participation in voluntary associations by party members.

There is a considerable body of evidence from previous research showing that both political participation and voluntary association participation are positively related to educational levels. For voluntary association participation, such findings are reported by Wright & Hyman (1958) and Hausknecht (1962, p. 17) in the U.S.A., and by Cauter & Downham (1954: p. 65) in their study of Derby. Milbrath (1965: ch. 5) has listed the

76 The Sociology of Grass Roots Politics

findings for political participation from a number of studies. These relationships are, of course, closely related to the relationship between social class and participation in associations. Attention is drawn to them here because they would indicate that the majority of people in each of the samples from Walton are those who are least likely, in terms of their educational background, to participate in the activities of voluntary associations. In this context the findings of Barnes (1967: pp. 122–4) in his study of the Italian Socialist Party that the effects of association memberships are most marked for those with the lowest educational levels are most interesting. He found that levels of political knowledge and political efficacy increased as the number of association memberships increased, but in each case the relationship was most strong for those with the lowest levels of educational achievements. Again because of the homogeneity in educational background of the groups studied here, comparable analysis has not been possible, but it may be considered that in the light of this and the other studies referred to, the evidence of the educational composition of the samples in Walton enhances the significance of the findings showing the relationship between party membership and voluntary association participation.

If the groups of both Labour and Conservative Party members and the electors in Walton are fairly homogeneous in terms of educational background, in terms of indices of housing standards they all appear quite heterogeneous. Housing standards were measured by a slightly modified version of Chapman's House Appraisal Schedule (1955). The schedule provides for the assessment of housing on a scale, and takes into account a wide range of housing standards, including household arrangements, size and number of rooms, type of housing, and state of repair of the property: it may be regarded as a useful indicator of social status in terms of standards of living and styles of life, though in that it is related to occupational class it is not altogether a pure measure of social status as opposed to social class. For analysis, the housing scores were arranged in five categories, ranging from very small unimproved nineteenth-century cottages which were characteristic of the first category, to the top category, which included only detached houses and superior modern semi-detached houses. Over two-thirds of the people in each group lived in housing of the third and fourth categories – the better type of pre-1914 property and post-1914 terraced and semi-detached houses. All categories of housing were found for all three groups, with the exception of the lowest category, which was not found for the Conservative group. Rank correlation analysis shows that Conservatives are more likely to live in housing of a higher category than either Labour members ($\gamma = 0.267$) or the electors ($\gamma = 0.326$), though in each case the relationship is not particularly large. There is virtually no difference, however, between the Labour members and electors.

If housing standards reflected the occupational-class composition of the groups, it would be expected that the housing standards of Labour members would tend to be lower than those of the electors: the reason why this is not so becomes apparent when the factor of home tenure is taken into consideration. As is shown in Table 4:5, over half the Labour members, compared with a third of the electors and one-fifth of the Conservatives, lived in corporation housing. The quality of this housing, most

Table 4:5 Home Tenure: Walton

	Lab. %	Cons. %	Electors %
Home owners	10·7	38·9	31·2
Corporation tenants	51·8	20·4	34·4
Tenants of private landlords*	37·5	40·7	34·4

of it low-density inter-war terraced and semi-detached property, is generally much better than most of the older property in the constituency. This housing achieves a relatively high score on the House Appraisal Schedule, and it is this which largely accounts for the fact that the housing standards of the Labour members are not below those of the electors, nor indeed much below those of the Conservatives.

* Those people who lived with their parents were included in this category, whether or not their parents were home owners.

The interest here in home tenure is twofold. Firstly home tenure is itself an index of social status, and also of social class in that home owners, corporation tenants and private tenants all have somewhat different economic interests. Secondly there is a fair amount of American evidence (Hausknecht, 1962: pp. 47–9: Wright & Hyman, 1958; Scott, 1957) indicating that people who own their homes are more likely to participate in the activities of voluntary associations than those who rent their homes. Milbrath (1965: p. 133) has indicated that people who own their own homes are more likely to participate in politics than those who are tenants. Hausknecht (1962) has suggested that home ownership is an index of integration in the local community: 'The young home owner ... is one for whom the mere fact of ownership of his home is tangible symbol of position and status within the community. His house serves to locate him, as it were, within the social system' (p. 49).

Looking at home tenure first as an index of class and status, Table 4:5 indicates that differences between the samples in incidence of home ownership very much reflect occupational-class differences; but as is the case for occupational class, all groups may be regarded as fairly heterogeneous in terms of this measure, though the Labour group is more homogeneous than the other two. Viewing home ownership as an index of social integration, it might be expected that in the light of previous findings indicating a relationship between this and voluntary association participation, party members would be more likely to be home owners than non-members. This was found to be the case in Church ward, where over 70 per cent of the Liberal Party members, compared with 44 per cent of the sample of electors, were home owners, the difference being at an acceptable level of statistical significance. In Walton, however, no such relationship is found. The proportion of home owners among the Labour group is much lower than that among the electors, and that the proportion is highest for the Conservatives would seem to be largely a reflection of socio-economic differences between the samples, rather than tangible evidence of a relationship between party membership and home ownership.

In any case the difference between the Conservatives and electors is not large.

In spite of this negative evidence the question of the relationship between home ownership and participation in the activities of other associations may be considered worth exploring, because party members who are association activists are multiple members of associations, and in terms of the theory of mass society multiple memberships are particularly important for social integration. The evidence from Church ward is that for both the Liberals and electors, association activists are more likely to be home owners than the non-participants. Again, however, the evidence from Walton is entirely negative: with all groups combined, slightly less than a quarter of the association activists compared with just over a quarter of the non-participants were home owners. The proportion of private tenants is somewhat higher among the association activists, and the proportion of corporation tenants very similar for both groups. Overall, the differences are so small as to justify the conclusion that there is no relationship between home tenure and participation in associations, and further analysis of the groups of Labour members, Conservatives and electors separately is rendered unnecessary.

The inconsistency between the findings for Church ward and Walton is not problematic when it is considered that there is a very close connection between home ownership as an index of class and status and as an index of social integration. First of all the American evidence that home owners are more likely to participate in associations than tenants must be considered against the facts that participation in associations in America is predominantly middle class. It is not sufficient to argue, as Hausknecht has done (1962: pp. 47–8), that the effect of home ownership is independent of class and status because it remains when factors of income and education are controlled: whatever other indices of class and status are controlled, home ownership itself remains an index of class and status. It is suggested here that where participation in associations is predominantly middle class, then, and only then, does the relationship between participation and home ownership hold. The relationship holds for the

Liberals in Church ward, because Church ward is a middle-class area, and the Liberal members, in terms of occupational class and education, are much more a middle-class group than either the Labour or Conservative Party members in Walton. The relationship is not found in Walton because this is much more a working-class area, and participation in voluntary associations there would not appear to be a predominantly middle-class activity. It may be remarked that as home ownership is characteristically middle class, then if the relationship between home ownership and participation in voluntary associations were general, the postulate that home ownership is indicative of social integration is not far removed from the notion that middle-class people are more integrated in their communities than working-class people. The ideological overtones implicit in this and related aspects of the theory of mass society are discussed in Chapter 6.

One reason given by Hausknecht for the assertion that home ownership is an index of integration is that home owners are likely to remain in the same neighbourhoods for longer periods than tenants. Whether or not this is so, it would seem reasonable to assume that the longer people have lived in a community, the more likely they are to be integrated. Milbrath's secondary analysis (1965: p. 133) indicates that the longer a person resides in a given community, then the greater is the likelihood of his participation in politics. In Walton it was found that party members tended to have lived at the same address for longer periods than the electors: just over 70 per cent of both the Labour and Conservative Party members had lived at the same address for more than fifteen years, in comparison with just 51 per cent of the electors. This would suggest that party members are drawn disproportionately from the more settled sectors of the community. No relationship was found, however, between length of residence and voluntary association activity.

Party Divisions and Political Attitudes

In this section the analysis of social and economic divisions relevant to party membership and voluntary association participation is supplemented by a consideration of political attitudes pertaining to class and party divisions. The particular attitudes considered here are those of self-assigned social class, and politico-economic attitudes measured along a radical/conservative continuum. Further, in an attempt to examine how far ideological differences are simultaneously superimposed upon class and party divisions, an analysis is given of the relationship between occupational class and both types of attitude.

At the outset it should be made clear that self-assigned social class is not regarded simply as the subjective counterpart of objective measures of social class. Dahrendorf (1959: pp. 145–7) has convincingly shown that there can be no pure subjective sociological concept of social class because, as a sociological concept, class must have some basis in the social structure. As a sociological concept, self-assigned class is more appropriately seen, as by Bott (1954), as an index of class imagery rather than as direct evidence of class structure and stratification. Having said this, it must be added that the notion of social class as employed here in terms of power and interests implies the recognition of these interests, and that somewhat similarly social stratification as a form of hierarchical order implies the recognition of criteria of status and prestige. Self-assigned class does, then, have some bearing upon both social class and stratification, though the relationship is very imprecise. Allardt (1964) has suggested that self-assigned class is identification of social strata rather than classes, reflecting status sensitivity rather than class consciousness.

The question used here for self-assigned social class was open-ended, because, as shown by Gross (1953), responses to a closed question, giving perhaps the categories of upper, middle and working class, or upper middle, lower middle and lower class, are likely to vary according to the categories used. The use of an open-ended question resulted in some variety of class labels being given by the people interviewed, but the most popular labels were middle, lower middle, working and lower class. It was possible to reduce all responses to two broad categories, those of middle and working class, leaving a residual category for those people not identifying with any social class. It is recognised, as Goldthorpe & Lockwood (1963) have noted, that the same class label may give rise to a number of different class images: a manual worker describing himself as middle class may see himself as belonging to the middle of the working class. The technique employed by Runciman (1964 and 1966) of asking the people interviewed to describe the sort of people who belong to the class with whom they have identified was

Table 4:6 Self-assigned Social Class: Walton

Category	Lab.	Cons.	Electors
Middle class	14	32	15
Working class	33	14	34
Don't know and not classifiable	9	8	12
	56	54	61

Table 4:7 Self-assigned Social Class: Walton
Rank Correlation Comparisons

	Values for* d	Values for d with proportions of manual and non-manual groups standardised
Conservatives: Labour	0·398	0·304
Conservatives: electors	0·376	0·256
Electors: Labour	0·008	0·048

repeated here. Unfortunately the number of criteria for class assessment employed was too large for any useful analysis. Furthermore, while some people were unable to articulate their ideas about the class structure, others clearly did not have any ideas of criteria for class assessment. As there was little difference between the members of the two parties and the electorate for these responses, attention here is confined to the class labels chosen, reduced to the categories of middle and working class.

* This asymmetric correlation coefficient is explained in the methodological appendix.

Party Divisions and Social Class 83

As might be expected, Table 4:6 shows that the majority of Labour members gave working-class responses, and most Conservatives gave middle-class responses, though the differences between the parties are much smaller than those recorded in the studies of Greenwich (Benney et al., 1956, p. 47) and Newcastle (Bealey et al., 1965, p. 254), and it may be considered that there is a considerable amount of overlap between the parties. With all three groups combined, the dependence of self-assigned class upon occupational class is expressed by the coefficient $d = 0.233$, showing the extent to which people classified as non-manual are more likely to give middle-class responses than those classified as manual. The relationship is not especially large, and, as shown in Table 4:7, with standardisation by occupational class the differences between the Conservatives and the other two samples remain substantial. It may also be noted that there is virtually no difference in class responses between the Labour members and electors.

Political attitudes along a radical/conservative continuum were measured in Walton by the responses, in terms of agreement with, disagreement with, or ambivalence to the following six statements:

1. Ordinary working people should be given more say in the running of industry.
2. Trade unions in this country have become too powerful and influential.
3. Economic recessions and trade slumps can be prevented by proper government planning.
4. No one should be able to earn more than £10,000 a year.
5. It is up to the government to make sure that everyone has a secure job and good standard of living.
6. Present laws favour the rich as against the poor.

Five of these questions were derived from the 'politico-economic conservatism' scales of Adorno et al. (1950: pp. 163–78) and the remaining question from the inventory of social attitudes devised by Eysenck (1954: p. 122). On the grounds of face validity, responses to these statements are regarded as indicating radical or conservative attitudes, but as employed here they are not intended to be projective, to indicate personality factors, or to indicate a single continuum of one basic underlying attitude. These statements and a number of others were tested on a non-random sample of forty people in South Liverpool, and the responses when intercorrelated in this and the Walton study were considered to reflect a sufficient degree of consistency to merit the construction of a scale: radical responses to one statement tended to be related to radical responses to all the others, and vice versa. An earlier series of statements employed in the study of Church ward had to be discarded because it failed to meet this test of consistency. The scale was constructed by assigning scores of minus one, nought, and plus one to radical, neutral and conservative responses for each individual statement, as has been done by Centers (1949), and summarising the scores in the form of a thirteen-point scale, ranging from minus six to plus six. The resulting scale is of very limited validity, simply indicating that a person with a high score has given more conservative responses to the six statements than a person with a low score; and because the responses to each of the statements are interrelated, then, comparatively, high-scoring persons may be considered conservative and low-scoring persons radical in terms of the attitudes covered by the questions. The scale is not an interval or even strictly an ordinal one, as it cannot really be claimed to reflect degrees of underlying attitudes of radicalism or conservatism. If this does not appear very satisfactory to the reader, it must be added that the author is persuaded by Sorokin's brilliant critique of apparently more sophisticated tests (1958) that their application would not be appropriate here.

The differences in the distribution of the scores on the thirteen-point scale, which for this analysis must be assumed to be ordinal, are summarised by the symmetric and asymmetric rank correlation coefficients given in Table 4:8.* The differences between the three groups are very large indeed, with the attitudes of the electors intermediate between those of the members of the two parties, though they are closer to the Conservatives than the Labour members. It should be noted that the coefficients

* A more detailed analysis of these data may be found in Chapter 6 and appendix IV of my M.A. thesis (1967).

refer to the probability that members of one group have a lower or more radical score than those of another group. This is very different from an indication of the extent to which each group is homogeneous in terms of attitudes. Some previous studies of party members in Britain have indicated that the level of consensus as to political opinions tends to be quite low for any one party: among Labour Party members in Manchester the level of consensus on questions of policy was found by Donnison & Plowman (1954) to be little above the chance level, and from a

Table 4:8 Scale of Radical/Conservative Attitudes: Walton Rank Correlation Comparisons

	Values for d	Values for γ
Labour:Conservatives	0·655	0·709
Labour:electors	0·358	0·399
Electors:Conservatives	0·289	0·321

study of Glossop, Plowman (1955) has reported a marked lack of consensus among Labour Party members on policy questions: in the same study the level of consensus among Liberal and more so among Conservative Party members was found to be much higher, though there was still considerable divergence from the 'party line'. The evidence here, which is of more general radical or conservative attitudes rather than those towards specific party policies, also indicates a fair amount of overlap between and lack of consensus within the parties.

The extent of this overlap is demonstrated by an analysis of the responses to each statement separately. The greatest amount of cleavage between the parties was reflected in the responses to the second statement, concerning the power of trade unions: 83 per cent of the Conservatives agreed with the statement, and 59 per cent of the Labour members disagreed with it. However, the only other statement for which both a majority of the Conservative members gave conservative responses and a majority of Labour members radical responses was the sixth. A substantial degree of consensus between the parties is reflected in the responses to the third and fifth statements, in each case the majority of the members of each party giving radical responses. Responses to the two remaining statements indicate the lack of consensus within the parties: less than half the Labour members gave radical responses to the fourth statement, and less than half the Conservative members gave conservative responses to the first statement.

Some further indication of overlap between the three groups is given by reducing the distributions of scores on the thirteen-point scale to the two categories of high scorers (conservatives) and low scorers (radicals), with the cutting point between the scores of nought and plus one. 20 per cent of the Labour members were classified as high scorers, and 32 per cent of the Conservatives as low scorers. As might be expected, the electors were fairly evenly balanced with a slight majority (56 per cent) classified as low scorers. The distinction between high scorers and low scorers is also useful for analysis of the relationship between radical or conservative attitudes and both self-assigned class and occupational class, to which attention is now turned. The evidence from Walton is that, with all groups combined, subjectively working-class people are more likely to be radical than subjectively middle-class people ($\gamma = 0.420$) and that the higher a person's occupational-class category, the less likely is he to express radical attitudes ($\gamma = 0.442$). In view of the nature of the statements given for the assessment of radical or conservative attitudes, reflecting to some extent class and economic interests, these correlations are not surprising. What is of particular interest is their variation in size between the different categories of respondents, because the extent to which these attitudes are superimposed upon self-assigned class assessments and occupational class may be regarded as indicating the extent of awareness of class interests, and therefore class consciousness. As is shown in Table 4:9, there are large variations between the different categories. The relationship between political attitudes and occupational class is strongest among the Labour group and weakest among the Conservatives. The relationship between self-assigned class and political attitudes is very strong among the Labour members, whereas it is very small for the electors, with a small negative relationship for the Conservatives:

subjectively working-class Conservatives are slightly less likely to be low scorers (radicals) than subjectively middle-class Conservatives. The evidence would suggest that Labour members are much more aware of social-class divisions than either the Conservatives or electors, and this would appear to be consistent with previous research findings that Labour members are more interested in politics than Conservatives (Benney et al., 1956: p. 49) and that Labour members have more political awareness than Conservatives or Liberals (Bealey et al., 1965: p. 295).

Table 4:9 Political Attitudes, Self-assigned Class and Occupational Class: Walton
Rank Correlation Comparisons: values for γ

	Attitudes and self-assigned class	Attitudes and occupational class
Labour members	0·689	0·444
Conservative members	−0·149	0·298
Electors	0·173	0·367

The superimposition of divisions in political attitudes upon self-assigned-class and occupational-class divisions may be taken to indicate that social class and status are very relevant to political party divisions. As was stated at the beginning of this chapter, this does not mean that the theory of mass society is less appropriate here than a deterministic class theory. That the memberships of the Labour and Conservative parties to some extent reflect different class interests means that these different interests are channelled through the political process and this may be regarded as conducive to democracy. In the first place, as argued in Chapter 1 (p. 28), if support for parties is class-based, this is likely to result in the integration of the working classes in the political process through party activity. This integration is also facilitated by participation in the activities of voluntary associations which is along the lines of party support: it has been shown in the previous chapter that multiple memberships of associations are to some extent superimposed along party lines. In the second place the superimposition of class and party divisions may be seen as reinforcing the differentiation and levels of conflict between the parties. Reference has been made in Chapter 1 (p. 25) to Dahrendorf's point that liberal democratic politics are the politics of conflict. Here it may be added that in terms of the theory of mass society the threat to democratic politics lies more in political apathy than in any notion of internecine class struggles; and that the maintenance of high levels of political interest and participation depends very much on the existence of substantial differences and conflicts between the parties. Some further comments on this point are made in the final chapter of this monograph, and here it will suffice to refer to the evidence of Campbell (1962) to the effect that where no important differences are seen between the alternative parties, political apathy is likely to result: also worth mentioning is the evidence from Scandinavia of Himmelstrand (1962) and Torgensen (1962) that the decline in ideological conflicts between the parties leads to a decline in political involvement.

In conclusion, it is necessary to return to the point made at the beginning of this chapter that, for the theory of mass society, pluralist democratic politics are not pure class politics, because they require the memberships of parties and associations to be heterogeneous in composition and multiple memberships to be cross-cutting in terms of class and other interests. It has been shown in this chapter that the parties studied are in fact fairly heterogeneous in social composition. The inference in the previous chapter that the incidence of cross-cutting memberships is sufficient to indicate the possibility of interlocking channels of communication has been supplemented by evidence that multiple memberships are not generally simultaneously superimposed upon party and class divisions. The superimposition of political attitudes upon self-assigned and occupational-class divisions is only relative, and the ideological differences revealed between the members of the different parties do not obscure a considerable lack of consensus within and overlap between the parties on these issues.

5 Politics, Communications and Social Attitudes

In the two previous chapters descriptions of the social and political participation of party members have been given, and the patterns of multiple memberships, in particular the extent to which these are superimposed upon, or overlap class, party and religious lines, have also been described. These chapters have described the extent of participation and how far the patterns of participation are in accordance with the conditions for social integration and democracy suggested by the theory of mass society. So far, however, no empirical consideration has been given to the question as to what in fact are the consequences of this social and political participation. Of course the consequences have been spelled out theoretically in the theoretical framework of the study set out in Chapter 1, but it would hardly be satisfactory to leave the matter at that. The theory of mass society posits that under certain conditions participation in the activities of parties and voluntary associations is conducive to social integration and democracy. This chapter attempts to provide some empirical substantiation for the notion that such participation does in fact contribute to social integration and democracy by examining the relationship between participation and a number of relevant social factors. These factors, in order of discussion, are those of self-designated opinion leadership, exposure to and interest in the mass media, and the expression of authoritarian attitudes. Previous research, to be referred to below, has indicated that all these factors are positively related to social and political participation, and it will be argued here that the first two factors may be regarded as indicators of social integration; while the expression of authoritarian attitudes may be regarded as contrary to democratic attitudes. In the previous two chapters, with the emphasis very much on the extent of cleavage between the parties, much of the analysis has been concerned with differences between the parties. Here, with the emphasis on the extent of social integration of party members, similarities between the parties are more important than differences. In fact the only significant differences between the parties in terms of the variables considered here occur in the expression of authoritarian attitudes, and therefore much of the analysis deals solely with differences between party members and non-members, without distinguishing the particular parties separately.

Before proceeding with the analysis, it should be made clear that the evidence put forward here falls far short of a testing of the postulates of the theory of mass society, and that the conclusions of the study must rely very much on theoretical inference. This is not to say that the theory of mass society is not in principle reducible to falsifiable propositions, but that the testing of such propositions requires empirical research on a much more extensive scale than that of the modest study here. An examination of the consequences of different patterns of association memberships and multiple memberships would require a detailed study of a substantial number of associations to enable comparisons between memberships of homogeneous and heterogeneous associations, and between actual multiple memberships which are superimposed and those which are overlapping. In order to include reasonable numbers of interlocking memberships which could be classified according to whether they were superimposed upon or cut across particular interests, it is likely that the number of associations studied would need to be quite large. Although there is a considerable body of research findings published which bears on the theory of mass society, the author is not aware of any direct attempt at verification as suggested here having been made. The interest here in multiple memberships is, of course, restricted to the voluntary association memberships of party members.

Opinion Leadership: interpersonal communication channels

Opinion leaders are people who are influential in their immediate face-to-face relationships. Lipset (1960: p. 196) and Hausknecht (1962: pp. 116–18) have noted the positive relationship between opinion leadership and membership of voluntary associations:

Rokkan (1959) and Lane (1959: p. 166) have demonstrated a similar relationship between political participation and opinion leadership. There are several possible explanations for this relationship. In the first place, as indicated by Katz & Lazarsfeld (1955: pp. 272–5), opinion leaders are found disproportionately among people of high status. For the U.S.A. at least, social status might therefore be a factor in explaining the relationship as it is also similarly related to voluntary association membership and political participation. Here, if the incidence of opinion leadership is much the same for the members of both the Labour and Conservative parties, then it would seem reasonable to discount factors of social status, such as education and occupation. More important is the fact that opinion leadership and participation in associations have a close theoretical link. As Katz & Lazarsfeld have put it: 'Almost by definition – for the idea of leader implies followers – it would be reasonable to postulate that persons who influence the opinions and habits of others are more likely to have a broader range of social contacts than non-opinion leaders' (1955: p. 227). The theory of mass society depends very much on the postulate that participation in associations also results in a wide range of social contacts for the members. Katz & Lazarsfeld (1955: pp. 287–9) have shown that gregariousness, as measured by numbers of friends and organisation memberships, is strongly related to opinion leadership. Broad ranges of social contacts are crucial in voluntary associations and for opinion leadership in so far as both operate as channels of communication and influence in society. In that opinion leaders may also be regarded as people with an above-average knowledge of and interest in social affairs, they may therefore be regarded as more likely to be socially integrated than non-opinion leaders.

For this study, self-designated opinion leadership has been measured by the responses to two questions derived from the study by Katz & Lazarsfeld:

1. Have you recently been asked for your advice about social or political affairs?
2. Compared with other people belonging to your circle of friends, are you more or less likely than most of them to be

92 The Sociology of Grass Roots Politics

asked for advice on what one should think on social or political matters?

In Church ward it was found that a much higher proportion of the Liberals than of the electors rated themselves as opinion leaders. The evidence for Walton is similar in that a higher proportion of party members than electors rated themselves as opinion leaders, but the proportion of opinion leaders among party members was much lower and, as is shown in Tables 5:1 and 5:2, the difference between party members and non-members is not very great. In both Church ward and Walton much higher proportions of association activists were found to be opinion leaders than non-activists. In Walton, with the three groups combined, the relationship between opinion leadership and

Table 5:1 Self-designated Opinion Leadership: Walton

	Lab.	Cons.	Electors
Rated leaders on both questions	9	7	4
Rated leaders on one question	15	12	17
Not rated on either question	31	30	40
	55	49	61

Table 5:2 Self-designated Opinion Leadership: Walton
Rank Correlation Comparisons

	Values for γ	Values for γ with proportion of association activists standardised
Labour:electors	0·220	0·062
Conservatives:electors	0·129	−0·013

association activity is very high, as expressed by the coefficient $\gamma = 0·691$. As is shown in the second column of Table 5:2, with the proportions of association activists in each sample standardised, the differences in the incidence of opinion leadership between party members and non-members are virtually eliminated. This may be taken as an indication that party members are more likely than non-members to be opinion leaders only in so far as they are more likely to participate in the activities of associations. It would, however, be wrong to assume that the relationship between party membership and opinion leadership should be discounted, because another way of putting this would be that party members are more likely to be opinion leaders because they have broader ranges of social contacts than non-members: the evidence that party members who are active for their parties are more likely to be association activists than passive members, discussed in Chapter 3 (p. 60), adds weight to the argument that the relationship between party membership and opinion leadership is not to be discounted because of the effects of the standardisation.

If opinion leadership depends partly on a broad range of social contacts, then it also depends partly on levels of information and interest. The issues on which opinion leaders are influential are presumably those in which they have considerable interest, and about which they have more information than the people they influence: this is one of the reasons why opinion leadership may be indicative of social integration. One index of levels of both information and interest is the degree of exposure to the mass media – newspapers, books, magazines, radio and television – and there is considerable evidence to show that opinion leaders are characterised by higher levels of exposure to the mass media than non-leaders (Katz & Lazarsfeld, 1955: pp. 310–16; Rogers, 1962: p. 238; Carter & Clarke, 1962). This evidence forms the basis of the American theory of mass communications to the effect that the influence of the mass media operates not directly upon the atomised masses, but largely through the face-to-face contacts of opinion leaders. In the next section the relationship between party membership and exposure to the mass media, taking into account both opinion leadership and activity in voluntary associations, is examined.

Newspapers, Radio and Television: mass communication channels

A high level of exposure to the mass media may be regarded as an indicator of social integration in that people who are more

94 The Sociology of Grass Roots Politics

exposed to the media are more likely to have more information about and to be more interested in social and political affairs. This is a somewhat broad generalisation, and subject to several possible exceptions, one example of which might be the indiscriminate viewing of one television channel for long periods each day: it is questionable as to whether this sort of high exposure to the mass media is related to knowledgeability, interest, and social integration. The limited interest in the mass media here does not warrant a discussion of this problem, and it must suffice here to note that evidence of exposure to the mass media has been limited to that which is likely to reflect knowledge about and interest in social and political affairs.

There is considerable evidence from previous research indicating a relationship between political and voluntary association participation and exposure to the mass media. Dahl's New Haven study (1961: p. 258) indicates that politically active citizens were more likely than the inactive to read the two local newspapers; the Finnish study of Allardt & Pesonen (1960) records a relationship between political participation and readership of two or more newspapers and three or more periodicals; and Barnes (1967) reports a similar relationship between exposure to newspapers and other sources of information and level of political participation amongst members of the Italian Socialist Party. For evidence on voluntary association participation, Cauter & Downham, in a study of Derby (1954: p. 211), have reported a positive relationship between club membership and readership of books, magazines and newspapers, and Allardt et al., in another Finnish study (1958), have noted a similar relationship between social participation and readership. Although here the concern is with newspaper readership rather than other forms of readership, it is perhaps also worth noting that Hausknecht's secondary analysis of American data reveals a relationship between membership of voluntary associations and readership of books and magazines (1962: pp. 91–5).

The evidence from this study refers to readership of individual daily newspapers, the numbers of newspapers read and reported interest in topics covered in the press and on radio and television programmes. Regular readership of daily newspapers was assessed by asking people which papers, if any, they read at least three times a week. In Church ward the most popular national daily for both the Liberals and electors was the *Daily Express*, reflecting the fact that this paper has the largest circulation among people with non-manual occupations, and echoing the findings from Newcastle (Bealey et al., 1965: p. 259) that Liberal Party members were more likely to read Conservative than Labour newspapers. Figures for the most popular papers reported read regularly in Walton are given in Table 5:3, and from this it is clearly apparent that party members generally read papers that are sympathetic to their own political parties.

Table 5:3 Readership of Daily Newspapers: Walton

	Lab.	Cons.	Electors
Right-wing national dailies			
Daily Mail	2	17	7
Daily Express	13	26	21
Left-wing national dailies			
Sun	18	0	4
Daily Mirror	28	5	21
Local dailies			
Liverpool Echo (evening)	50	46	47
Liverpool Daily Post (morning)	7	5	2
	n = 56	n = 54	n = 61

The proportions of Conservatives reading the *Daily Mail* and *Daily Express* correspond closely to the proportions of Labour members reading the *Sun* and the *Daily Mirror*. This is, of course, very much to be expected, and is consistent with similar findings by Bealey et al. (1965: pp. 258–9). In comparing the two parties it is also noteworthy that the Labour members are much more likely to read right-wing newspapers than the Conservatives are to read left-wing ones. This is consistent with the findings of Milne & Mackenzie (1956: p. 96) from Bristol that fewer left-wing papers were read by Conservative voters than right-wing papers by Labour voters. Lipset (1960: p. 205) has cited this and similar evidence from Scandinavia as evidence that working-class people are subject to greater cross-pressures than middle-class people, and, with the thesis that cross-pressures are conducive to political apathy, given this as one reason for the lower levels of voting for working-class people in comparison with the middle classes. This argument, mentioned in Chapter 1 (p. 24), will not be paid further attention at this point, and here it will simply be noted that in terms of the influence of the media, Labour Party members would appear more likely to be subject to cross-pressures than Conservatives.

Another piece of evidence to be noted from Table 5:3 is the somewhat greater incidence of readership of local newspapers among the party members than among the electors. The differences are not large, but are somewhat disguised in the table because the *Echo*, the only evening newspaper in Liverpool, is read by a large majority in each group, and conversely the

Table 5:4 Numbers of Daily Newspapers Read: Walton

	Lab.	Cons.	Electors
Three or more	19	8	9
Two	27	32	31
One	7	12	16
None	3	2	5
	56	54	61

Daily Post is read by only a small minority in each group. If readership of local papers is taken as an indication of interest in local community affairs, then this is evidence, admittedly slight, that party members are more interested in local affairs than non-members. When it is considered that the local parties are much more centred on local government and local elections, this is not very surprising. The findings from Church ward are similar in that a higher proportion of Liberals than electors were readers of the *Daily Post*. For comparison here, the evidence of Dahl (1961: pp. 257–8) from New Haven that politically active citizens were more likely to read both local newspapers may be referred to.

Turning now to the evidence of numbers of daily newspapers that are read regularly, Tables 5:4 and 5:5 indicate that party

Politics, Communications and Social Attitudes 97

members are more likely to read more newspapers than non-members. The differences between the parties are also quite considerable, as the incidence of readership among the Labour members is much higher than among the Conservatives, for whom the incidence of readership is not much above that for the electors. It would appear that the fact that Labour members

Table 5:5 Number of Daily Newspapers Read: Walton Rank Correlation Comparisons*

	Values for γ	Values for γ with proportions of men and women standardised	Values for γ with proportions of association activists standardised
Labour:electors	0·415	0·381	0·331
Conservatives:electors	0·140	0·208	0·040
Labour:Conservatives	0·336	0·222	0·348

are more cross-pressured than the Conservatives in that they read more left-wing papers than the Conservatives do right-wing ones is explicable in that the Labour members read more papers than the Conservatives: as shown in Table 5:3, left-wing dailies are just as popular with Labour members as are right-wing dailies with Conservatives. Some of the difference in incidence of readership might be accounted for in that the majority of the Conservatives interviewed were women, and most of the Labour members men. This is in fact the case, for with all groups combined, the probability of men reading more newspapers than women is expressed by the coefficient $\gamma = 0·362$. However, although standardisation of the proportions of men and women, as shown in the second column of Table 5:5, increases the difference between the Conservatives and the electors, and reduces the differences between the Labour group and both the Conservatives and electors, the difference between the Labour and Conservative members remains substantial.

In the previous section it was noted that activity in voluntary

* For computation of these values it has been necessary to put in one category the responses of people who reported reading one newspaper and those reporting no regular readership.

associations was strongly related to opinion leadership, more so in fact than party membership. Here, evidence of the relationship between newspaper readership and activity in associations discloses a much weaker link, though one that is still of sufficient size to be interesting. The probability that association activists read more newspapers than non-participants is described by the coefficient $\gamma = 0.245$. As shown in Table 5:5, standardisation of proportions of association activists substantially reduces the difference between the Labour members and electors, and virtually eliminates the difference between the Conservatives and electors, though it should be noted that this standardisation does not simultaneously take into account the standardisation of the sexes.

For inferring levels of knowledge and interest from exposure to the mass media, it must be recognised that the index of numbers of newspapers read is somewhat crude, because readership of one 'quality' newspaper is likely to give more knowledge than readership of two of the more popular sensational papers. To provide a more sensitive indication of exposure to the mass media, the people interviewed were given check-lists of topics and asked whether they were interested in reading about such topics in the papers they read or listening to programmes concerned with them on the radio or television. The resulting evidence is, of course, highly subjective and cannot be regarded as a direct indicator of exposure to the media as can the number of newspapers read. It is very useful, however, because it may be taken as a direct indicator of interest, and it is assumed here that if people are interested in particular things then they are likely to read about them in the papers and listen to radio and television programmes about them. The subjectivity of the material means that the reported levels of interest may be inflated in order to impress the interviewer, and indeed one would think this to be quite likely. This does not really present any problem here because the concern is solely with difference between the different groups. It may be added that subjective data often has the advantage of taking into account the individual's own perspective, his 'definition of the situation', which is very relevant to his behaviour, and, after all, the question of interest in social and political affairs is in principle a subjective one. Rogers (1962: p. 230) has put forward a similar argument in defence of the self-designating technique of assessing opinion leadership, the technique which has been employed in this study.

Three check-lists of topics were used, two for newspapers and one for radio and television. The two lists referring to newspapers contained mostly the same topics, but were each intended to gauge a different type of orientation: for the first list people were asked about their interest in events, whereas for the second they were asked whether they were interested in reading about the people involved in social and political affairs. The first list, concerning news of events, contained the following nine topics:

1. National government
2. Local government.
3. Conservative Party.
4. Labour Party.
5. Liberal Party.
6. Research, science and education.
7. Trade unions.
8. Industry.
9. Foreign affairs (not disasters, etc.).

The second list, concerning news about people, contained all except the sixth and seventh topics from the first list together with three additional topics: 8. Royal family; 9. Television personalities; 10. Television, film and stage stars. Only the response to the first of these three topics is considered here, and this is dealt with separately. The other two topics were included solely to broaden the coverage of the list, and are of no interest here. When presented with the second list, the people interviewed were asked specifically if they were interested in reading about the work activities of the people in each category. In the Church ward study a further list, referring to interest in news about the leisure activities of people in each category, was also used, but was discarded for the Walton study because the reported levels of interest were generally very low: this probably means that people do not like admitting to university interviewers that they enjoy reading gossip columns in the popular press rather than anything more significant. The third list, for interest in topics covered on radio and television programmes

100 The Sociology of Grass Roots Politics

was similar to the first, but included only six categories instead of nine: the trade union category was dropped, and only one category given for political parties.

The distribution of the responses for each category between the groups of party members and electors was very similar for each list, except in that interest expressed in news about people was generally much lower than that in news of events. In Church ward it was found that for almost every topic on all three lists, a much higher proportion of the Liberals than the electors reported interest in reading or listening. Similarly, in Walton, for nearly every topic on each list, a much higher proportion of the party members than of the electors reported interest. Before

Table 5:6 Reported Interest in Newspaper, Radio and Television Topics: Walton
Rank Correlation Comparisons: values for γ

	Newspaper topics		Radio and television topics
	News of events	News about people	
Party members: non-members	0·301	0·286	0·285
Party members: non-members (non-participants only)	0·214	0·186	0·147
Association activists: non-participants	0·456	0·423	0·375
Opinion leaders: non-leaders	0·407	0·365	0·439
Labour: Conservatives	0·023	0·037	0·139

considering these differences in more detail, a few remarks must be made about the differences between the responses of the Labour and Conservative members. It is rather stating the obvious to note that party members were much more interested in their own parties than any others, but it is noteworthy that members of both parties were much more interested in the Liberal Party than the electors. Labour members were much more interested than Conservatives in both trade unions and industry, explicable in the close connection of trade unions with the Labour Party, and the proportions of men and people with manual occupations in the Labour group in comparison with the

Conservative group. Somewhat more Conservatives than Labour members were interested in research, science and education, and a much higher proportion of Conservatives were interested in the royal family: in fact, the royal family was the most popular of the topics concerning news about people among the Conservatives. It might be expected that Conservative Party members would be more strongly monarchist than Labour members, but this should not be taken to indicate that attitudes to the royal family are a basis for cleavage between the parties. Nearly two-fifths of the Labour members did express interest in reading about the royal family, and a number of those who did not pointed out that they nevertheless approved of the royal family.

Table 5:7 Voluntary Association Activity and Interest in the Mass Media: Walton
Rank Correlation Comparisons: values for γ

	Newspaper topics News of events	News about people	Radio and television topics
Labour members	0·477	0·532	0·649
Conservative members	0·471	0·327	0·143
Electors	0·254	0·231	0·084

This piece of evidence would appear to be consistent with the thesis of Shils & Young (1953) that the monarchy is one basis for consensus in British society, though issue will be taken with this and other consensus theories of British politics in the concluding chapter (pp. 129–33). No further differences of any consequence were found between the parties, and attention is now turned to the analysis of differences between party members and non-members, and the effects of the variables of voluntary association activity and opinion leadership.

The correlation coefficients given in Table 5:6 show the relationship between the numbers of topics in which interest was reported and party membership, voluntary association

102 The Sociology of Grass Roots Politics

activity and opinion leadership. On each of the three lists, party members tended to report interest in more topics than the electors, and though the values for the differences between party members and the electors may not appear to be very large, it should be taken into account that the statistic γ here is a very sensitive measure, being computed from tables with between seven and ten ranks, ranging from interest expressed in none of the topics to interest in all nine, seven and six topics respectively for the three lists. As is shown by the third row of figures, with all three groups combined for analysis, voluntary association activists were likely to report interest in more topics than non-participants: moreover, for all three lists of topics, the relationship with the variable of association activity is much stronger than for party membership. This might suggest that it is the higher levels of voluntary association activity among the party members which account for the relationship between party membership and levels of interest. The complexity of the data prevents the use of the technique of standardising the proportions of association activists between the party members and electors to show altogether how far this is the case, but the figures in the second row suggest that the relationship between party membership and levels of interest remains substantial independent of the levels of voluntary association activity: comparing only those party members and electors who are not association activists, the party members are still somewhat more likely to express interest in more topics than the electors. The fourth row of figures shows the relationship between opinion leadership and levels of interest in topics, and although there are variations between the individual lists of topics, the relationship is generally of the same strength as that for association activists. This might in part reflect the strong relationship between voluntary association activity and opinion leadership, but may also be taken as confirmation of the postulate that opinion leaders have above-average knowledge of and interest in public affairs. The smallness of the differences in levels of interest between the two parties, shown in the final row of figures, justifies the combination of the two party samples for analysis.

The interpretation of this rather formidable array of correlation coefficients is very much helped by the evidence given in Table 5:7. So far it has been noted that party members were generally more interested in topics in the mass media than the electors, and that association activists were similarly more interested than those who were not association activists. It would seem to follow from this that party members who are association activists are likely to have higher levels of interest in the topics in the mass media than those who are not activists. Table 5:7 not only shows this to be the case, but also indicates that the relationship between association activity and levels of interest in the mass media is somewhat stronger among party members, particularly those of the Labour Party, than among the electors. This is of considerable theoretical importance, because party members who are association activists are multiple members of associations: multiple memberships may therefore be seen as strongly related to interest in and exposure to the mass media.

Authoritarian Attitudes

A central part of the theoretical framework of this study is the notion, expounded in Chapter 1, that participation in secondary associations which are heterogeneous in social composition and cross-cutting multiple memberships broaden the social perspective of the individual and are thus conducive to tolerant, non-authoritarian and democratic attitudes. In the two previous chapters it has been established that the parties are fairly heterogeneous in social composition and that the incidence of cross-cutting memberships is sufficient to indicate interlocking communication channels. In the above sections of this chapter it has been shown that opinion leadership and exposure and interest in the mass media are positively related to party membership and activity of party members in voluntary associations. This may be taken to indicate that party members, particularly those defined as voluntary association activists, have access to or are involved in more channels of communication than non-members: this in turn would indicate that party members, particularly those who are multiple members, are more integrated, have broader ranges of social contacts and broader social perspectives than non-members. It is therefore to be expected that a positive relationship would be found between both party membership and voluntary association activity, and tolerant, non-authoritarian and democratic attitudes.

There is a fair amount of evidence from previous research indicating that this is the case. Milbrath & Klein (1962) have reported from a small-scale study in Washington a negative correlation between a scale of authoritarianism (F Scale) and all types of political activity. In a critical analysis of much German literature on political participation, Dahrendorf (1968a: ch. 21) indicates that political apathy is related to authoritarian attitudes. Barnes (1967: pp. 175–6) found that the higher the level of participation in the Italian Socialist Party, the more likely were the members to accept a 'Classical' conception of democracy (i.e. in terms of participation and influence). Kornhauser (1960: p. 72) has produced evidence from a national sample of American workers to show a relationship between membership of voluntary associations and non-authoritarian attitudes. Arnold Rose (1962) found organisational leaders in Minnesota to be less prejudiced, and more favourable to civil rights, than the population at large. Finally attention may be drawn to the findings of Stouffer in another American national survey (1955) to the effect that community leaders are more tolerant of nonconformity than the mass of the population.

In Walton the expression of authoritarian attitudes was assessed by the responses, in terms of agreement, disagreement with, or ambivalence to the following three statements:

1. What young people need most of all is strict discipline by their parents.
2. What this country needs most, more than laws and political programmes, is a few strong, tireless and devoted leaders.
3. Sex crimes, such as rape and attacks on children, should be punished by flogging.

These three statements were among ten devised from the third form of the F Scale constructed by Adorno et al. (1950: p. 255) and a similar scale employed by Campbell et al. (1954: p. 225), which, with suitable alterations to the wording, were tested on a non-random sample of 40 persons in South Liverpool. Five of the statements proved to be unsatisfactory, and two of the remaining five questions employed in Walton have also had to be excluded from the analysis because of the grossly skewed distribution of the responses. On the grounds of face validity, agreement with the remaining three statements may be viewed as the expression of authoritarian attitudes. In both the South Liverpool pilot study and in Walton, intercorrelated responses to the three statements were considered to reflect a sufficient degree of consistency to merit the construction of a scale: agreement with one statement was positively related to agreement with the other two, and vice versa. A scale has been constructed by assigning scores of minus one, nought and plus one for liberal, neutral and authoritarian responses and summarising the scores in the form of a seven-point scale, ranging from minus three to plus three. The logic of the construction of the scale is the same as for the scale of radical/conservative attitudes discussed in Chapter 4, and the scale is therefore subject to the same limitations. It is in no way claimed to indicate underlying authoritarian personality traits, let alone an authoritarian personality syndrome, but simply provides a convenient means of summarising the incidence of *prima facie* authoritarian responses. It may be added that no relationship was found between authoritarian responses and conservative responses on the radical/conservative scale, reflecting the findings of Anderson et al. (1965) that supposed component factors of the authoritarian/conservative personality syndrome, as suggested by McClosky (1958) and others, were not in fact related to each other.

Apart from the limitations of the scale by virtue of its method of construction, it must be admitted that the authoritarian attitude scale employed here is subject to several weaknesses. In the first place, dependent on only three statements, the range of attitudes covered is very narrow. Furthermore, in that for each statement agreement constitutes an authoritarian response, the scale is subject to a response set: the evidence may be distorted by the tendency of some people to agree with or, less likely, disagree with everything that is put to them. From the point of view of empirical analysis, the most serious weakness of the scale is that the scores are heavily skewed towards the 'authoritarian' pole: the majority of people from all groups in Walton gave authoritarian responses to all three questions. Of course, it might just be the case that most people interviewed were authoritarians, but questionnaire responses to attitude statements cannot be regarded as valid evidence for this: objective assessments of any group in terms of such responses can be made only by comparisons with the responses of another group, and such comparative analysis is most fruitful where overall the responses are more or less evenly balanced between the opposite, in this case authoritarian and liberal, poles. To overcome these weaknesses, preliminary fieldwork and analysis would have been necessary on a scale far beyond the resources of the study. Their presence means that the index of authoritarian attitudes is somewhat crude, but by no means invalid: that the scores on the scale are related to the variables of age, sex, education and social class in the same way as has been found in previous studies, to be mentioned below, may be taken as confirmation of its validity.

Table 5:8 Scale of Authoritarian/Liberal Attitudes: Walton Rank Correlation Comparisons

	Values for d	Values for γ
Labour:Conservatives	0·318	0·450
Labour:electors	0·315	0·459
Conservatives:electors	0·006	0·011

The figures in Table 5:8 indicate that Labour members were much less likely than either the Conservatives or the electors to express authoritarian attitudes, there being virtually no difference between the latter two groups. In order to take into account the relationship between authoritarian attitudes and a number of relevant factors, the distribution of scores on the scale has been reduced to the simple dichotomy of high scorers (authoritarian) and low scorers (liberal): those with scores not

Politics, Communications and Social Attitudes

above plus one were classified as low scorers, and the remainder as high scorers, a high cutting-point being necessary because of the extent to which the scores were skewed towards the 'authoritarian' pole. This division clearly illustrates the differences between the Labour members and the other two groups: just over 70 per cent of both the Conservatives and electors were high scorers, in comparison with 46 per cent of the Labour members. The correlation coefficients reflecting these differences are given in the first row of Table 5:9, and that they are smaller than those in the previous table is explicable in that the collapsing of the range of scores to a dichotomy results in a higher proportion of ties between the groups of respondents.

Table 5:9 Scale of Authoritarian/Liberal Attitudes: Walton Standardised Rank Correlation Comparisons: values for d

	Labour: Conservatives	Labour: electors	Conservatives: electors
Unstandardised comparisons	0·277	0·232	−0·045
Proportions of men and women, and persons over and under 50 years of age standardised	0·162	0·201	0·039
Occupational class standardised	0·359	0·236	−0·123
Comparison for those with secondary modern or elementary school education only	0·333	0·338	0·024
Proportions of association activists standardised	0·253	0·171	−0·082

There is considerable evidence that the variables of age, sex, education and social class are related to authoritarian attitudes, and because there are significant differences between the three groups in Walton in terms of these variables they must be considered here. From the study of an American national sample, Stouffer (1955) found that women, older people and the less educated were less likely to be tolerant of nonconformity than men, younger people and the better educated. Bettelheim

& Janowitz (1964: ch. 1), drawing on the evidence of a number of empirical studies, have also indicated that younger people and the better educated are likely to be more tolerant and less prejudiced. That working-class people tend to be more authoritarian than middle-class people has been discussed in some depth by Lipset (1960: ch. 4). Lipset's thesis is of some theoretical relevance to this study, and is considered critically in the next chapter. Here the concern is chiefly with the empirical correlation of indices of social class with authoritarian attitudes, though it may be mentioned that there is evidence to suggest that this relationship is very much a function of educational differences (Lipsitz, 1965).

In Walton the relationship between authoritarian attitudes and each of the variables of age, sex, education and social class was found to be consistent with these previous findings, providing, apart from anything else, some confirmation of the validity of the scale employed. With the groups combined, that older people and women are more likely to express authoritarian attitudes is indicated by the respective coefficients of $d = 0.214$ and $d = 0.295$. Simultaneous standardisation by these two variables, as is shown in the second row of figures in Table 5:9, has the effect of considerably reducing the difference between the Labour and Conservative groups, and also slightly reducing the difference between the Labour members and electors. The electors appear now marginally more authoritarian than the Conservatives, a reverse of the unstandardised relationship, but in each case the difference is negligible. Turning to social class, the probability that people classified as manual are more authoritarian than those classified as non-manual is expressed by the coefficient $d = 0.173$. The relationship here is not very great, but is not so small as to be discounted. Standardisation by occupational class, as shown in the third row of figures in Table 5:9, has the effect of considerably increasing the difference between the Labour and Conservative groups and making the Conservatives appear significantly more authoritarian than the electors, a result somewhat the opposite of the previous standardisation. Education proved to be more strongly related to authoritarian attitudes than any of the other variables considered here, in that the higher the category of school last attended,* the less likely were people to express authoritarian attitudes, as shown by the coefficient $d = 0.324$. As most people in each group had attended secondary modern or elementary schools, standardisation was not practicable, but the fourth row of figures in Table 5:9 shows that the differences both between the Labour and Conservative members, and between the Labour members and electors, are considerably larger for people who have attended secondary modern or elementary schools than overall. In general the preceding analysis may be seen to emphasise the negative relationship between Labour Party membership and authoritarian attitudes, and to confirm that no real difference exists between the Conservative Party members and the electors. The negative relationship between party membership and authoritarian attitudes expected in terms of the theory of this study thus holds only for the Labour Party.

According to the theory of mass society, it would be the party members who are multiple members of associations who are the less authoritarian because of their broader ranges of social contacts and broader social perspectives. It is therefore to be expected that voluntary association activists would be less authoritarian than non-participants, and that this is in fact the case is indicated by the correlation coefficient, for all groups combined, of $d = 0.237$. The relationship is by far the strongest among Labour members ($d = 0.364$), but very slight among the Conservatives, and a comparison between the parties shows that association activists among Labour members are much less likely to be authoritarian than activists among the Conservatives ($d = 0.439$). As is shown in the final row of figures in Table 5:9, the only marked effect of standardisation of proportions of association activists is to reduce the difference between the Labour members and the electors. For the Labour members, then, the findings are exactly as predicted in terms of the theory of mass society: not only are they less likely than non-members to express authoritarian attitudes, but also the incidence of such attitudes is lower for the multiple members among them. It is not perhaps altogether surprising, in view of certain aspects of

* The three categories are listed in Table 4:3, above, p. 73.

110 The Sociology of Grass Roots Politics

Conservative Party ideology, such as emphasis on leadership, that the Conservative members should appear more authoritarian than Labour members on the scale employed here. It is something of a paradox that in terms of this and the measures of exposure to and interest in the mass media the Labour members more closely fit the theory of mass society than the Conservatives, although in Walton they are characterised by lower levels of party activity than the Conservatives. Most interesting for our theoretical conclusion to follow in the next and final chapter is the fact that membership of the working-class party more closely fits the theory of mass society than membership of the middle-class party, although it is often claimed, as by Perrow (1964), that the theory is appropriate only for middle-class political participation!

6 Theory and Problems of Grass Roots Politics

The starting-point of this study has been the assumption that grass roots political participation apart from merely voting is a necessary component for a democratic society. Membership of political parties and participation in the activities of voluntary associations are the forms of such grass roots participation selected for appraisal in this monograph, and a theoretical perspective under the name of the theory of mass society has been developed in order to show some of the more important consequences of this participation for the political system. In the preceding chapters the evidence from an empirical study of party membership, and the voluntary association participation of party members, carried out in Liverpool has been analysed in terms of this theoretical perspective. The reader is entitled to expect the final chapter of a monograph of this nature to draw together some conclusions from the empirical material, but this represents only a small part of the scope of this chapter, as the direct theoretical implications of the findings have been already explained. A brief summary of the empirical conclusions of the study is followed by a re-examination of the theoretical approach; for in addition to some questions thrown up by the empirical material, there are several other issues, such as the ideological implications of the theory, which have been raised but left suspended in preceding theoretical exposition. In conclusion the discussion leaves the theoretical plane for the forum of practical politics, and an attempt is made to relate the empirical and theoretical conclusions to some of the problems of democracy in contemporary British society.

Empirical Conclusions

The study has confirmed that party members are characterised by generally low levels of party political activity, but against this overwhelming evidence has been produced showing that party

112 The Sociology of Grass Roots Politics

members are much more likely to be active in voluntary associations than non-members: in a broad sense, therefore, party members are characterised by much higher levels of political participation than is revealed by an analysis restricted to party activities. Party members who participate in other associations are multiple members of associations, and while this may be a truism, it is of considerable theoretical importance. It is the strength of multiple memberships of associations and the extent to which these are overlapping rather than superimposed upon conflicting interests in society that is significant in maintaining social integration and democracy. Very much related to the condition of overlapping multiple memberships are the conditions that the membership of individual associations should be heterogeneous in social composition and that each association should require only partial, limited levels of commitment from its members and exercise a limited measure of control over them. Political participation under these conditions provides communication links between different interest groups in society and broadens the range of social contacts and thus the social perspective of the individual participants: both processes may be regarded as functional for social integration and democracy. It has been taken for granted that the parties studied achieve only partial and limited levels of commitment and control: indeed, in view of the low levels of party activity, the problem would seem to be one of ensuring adequate levels of political commitment, rather than any restriction. In Chapter 4 it has been shown that, notwithstanding strong social-class differences and ideological differences related to economic and class interests, the parties may be seen as fairly heterogeneous. Whether or not the other voluntary associations in which the party members participate are also characterised by partial commitment and control and heterogeneous memberships is an empirical question which cannot be answered here as no more has been done than to list the memberships of such associations. It is reasonable to assume for the argument here that by and large these conditions are met within most voluntary associations at least as far as they are within the political parties, though some exceptions would be expected: the social heterogeneity of trade unions is clearly

Theory and Problems of Grass Roots Politics 113

very limited, and some religious organisations, such as the Roman Catholic Church, may be regarded as seeking total commitment from and control over their members.

The pattern of multiple memberships of associations for party members has proved to be not altogether consistent with the model of overlapping memberships, because considerable evidence has emerged of superimposition of trade union and church memberships along party lines; and given the social-class differences between the Labour and Conservative parties it would be reasonable to infer a tendency for multiple memberships to be superimposed along party, class and religious lines. On the other hand, it has been possible to demonstrate the existence of a limited but not insignificant number of overlapping memberships, and correlation analysis has not confirmed that association memberships are simultaneously superimposed along the lines of class and party. It has therefore been concluded that the incidence of overlapping memberships disclosed may be taken as sufficient to indicate interlocking channels of communication between associations and interest groups, preventing their isolation from one another. At the same time, as in absolute numbers more memberships appear superimposed than overlapping, the pattern of multiple memberships may be regarded as more conducive to the enhancement of cleavage in society than to the development of consensus and reduction of conflict. This does not invalidate the theoretical approach because the reduction of conflict and spread of consensus are not regarded as having any necessary connection with social integration and democracy. The problem does remain, however, as to whether a set of multiple memberships superimposed along interests and social divisions does broaden an individual's range of social contacts and his social perspective, because it has been theorised that superimposed multiple memberships are more likely to reinforce prejudices. The answer to this might be that for the individual a set of superimposed memberships may still result in a broadened social perspective if the associations are heterogeneous and contain some members who do have a cross-cutting set of memberships whom he is likely to meet.

In Chapter 5 the relationship between political participation, communications and authoritarian attitudes has been examined in order to see whether this is consistent with our theoretical propositions as to the consequences of political participation. Now evidence of statistical correlations derived from instantaneous social surveys of the type employed here is not in itself evidence of causal relationships, and any conclusions in terms of the consequences of political participation must depend upon theoretical inference. With this qualification, that party members and voluntary association activists are more likely to be opinion leaders, to read more newspapers and show more interest in public issues disseminated through the mass media may be taken to indicate that political participation is conducive to the broadening of access to channels of communication, heightened political interest and awareness and social integration. The correlations are particularly strong for party members who are association activists, providing some confirmation for the theoretical proposition as to the importance of multiple memberships, but at the same time the notion that the apparent effects of party membership are explicable solely in terms of the high level of voluntary association participation among party memmembers, meaning that party membership *per se* is of little consequence, has been rejected: most of the correlations hold for party membership even with the proportions of association activists standardised, and for those that do not it should be considered that a substantial relationship has been found between voluntary association activity and party political activity.

The relationship between political participation and the expression of authoritarian attitudes has proved somewhat ambiguous. Labour members are much less likely to express such attitudes than non-members, and association activists have been found to be less authoritarian than non-participants, but on this variable there is no real difference between Conservative members and the electors. On balance, and taking into account the limitations of this particular piece of evidence, this does not add up to a refutation of the thesis of the contribution of party membership *per se*, to social integration and democracy, though it is certainly the case that the findings for the Labour Party members are more congruent with the theory of mass society than those for the Conservatives. This, however, enhances rather than detracts from the relevance of the theory to grass roots British politics: it is the Labour Party which is the main avenue for working-class participation, and it would seem reasonable to regard the integration of the working classes in the political process as more problematic than that of the middle classes.

In Chapter 2 Walton and Church ward were designated as working-class and middle-class areas respectively. The attention devoted to Liberal Party members in Church ward has been very limited because the empirical study in this ward amounted to no more than a small-scale pilot survey, but it has sufficed to show a marked degree of consistency for the findings between the two areas. The Liberal sample proved the most strongly middle class of the three parties studied, and it is possible that a more detailed study would have shown that this group more closely fitted the theoretical model than the other two. Indications of this are the strong relationships found between Liberal Party membership and opinion leadership and home ownership. It has been suggested, however, that this latter relationship is only likely to be found for middle-class participation in middle-class areas.

Theoretical Perspective: a reappraisal

In Chapter 1 (p. 28) the claim was made that the theory of mass society is of just as much validity for the examination of class-based political participation as for political participation which is not class-based. The point of this claim was to establish that a theory developed very much both in and for America might nevertheless be applicable to a study of political participation in Britain, and the empirical findings reported here have provided ample justification for this. The theory would seem equally applicable to both middle-class and working-class political participation and, in view of the findings for Labour Party members, if anything more appropriate to the latter. This may be taken as a refutation of Perrow's (1964) claim that the theory of mass society is applicable only to the middle and upper

116 The Sociology of Grass Roots Politics

classes in society, but this critique still merits some attention here. It is largely based on the evidence of a number of studies that political participation and voluntary association are predominantly middle-class activities. This pattern is likely to be less pronounced where political parties are class-based, because working-class parties provide avenues for working-class political participation, whereas parties which are ostensibly not class-based are likely to be predominantly middle class and provide few opportunities for working-class participation. Even so, in parties that rely on working-class support, for each higher level of participation, the proportion of working-class in contrast to middle-class participants declines. Barnes (1967: p. 96) has noted the over-representation of the middle class among the leadership in proportion to the party membership, and a strong relationship between political participation and social class among the membership of the Italian Socialist Party. More striking, only 30 per cent of British Labour M.P.s in 1966 could be described as working class (Richard Rose, 1968). Furthermore, even if to a lesser degree in Britain than America, it is beyond dispute that the level of working-class political participation is very low.

These facts may be unpalatable to sociologists and political scientists of more than one political persuasion, but they do not invalidate our theoretical proposition regarding the general consequences of participation for social integration and democracy. At the same time it is clearly inadequate to attempt to explain the maintenance of order and consensus in society through the existence of cross-cutting associational ties when large sectors of the population just do not have these ties. It is therefore only when social integration and democracy is equated with order, harmony and consensus that the theory of mass society becomes applicable only to the middle and upper classes in society. This equation has been carefully avoided in the theoretical approach to this study, but because certain mass society theorists, such as Kornhauser (1960: p. 80), are concerned with the effects of cross-cutting ties for the development of consensus and reduction of conflict, some further discussion is called for.

The notions of order, harmony and consensus are in fact related to the theory of mass society in rather a complicated way, and the unravelling of this relationship takes us to the ideological roots of the theory of mass society. These roots, as Bramson (1961: p. 30) has shown, are those of nineteenth-century romanticism with its idealisation of the organic folk community. The organic folk community, which is probably more accurately placed in mythology than history, was a society of harmony and order, characterised by natural *Gemeinschaft* relationships instead of the artificial *Gesellschaft* relationships of modern industrial society, if one may be permitted to use what Dahrendorf (1968a: pp. 128 and 300) has rightly described as a miserable, misleading, misinformed and illiberal dichotomy of German ideology. The organic folk community was also, it should be added, a rigid, oppressive, authoritarian and totally unfree society. Certain mass society theorists have thus been very concerned with social disorganisation and the problem of order in modern industrial society. The strengthening of neighbourhood, local community and voluntary association ties within the city have been seen as means of combating the 'evils' of the city such as anonymity, alienation, *anomie* and personal disorganisation (Arnold Rose, 1954: ch. 2). The anti-urban value orientation, embodying the quite unfounded assumption that most people hate cities and really want to live in idyllic village communities, which is implicit here may also be traced to nineteenth-century romanticism. Kornhauser (1960: p. 77) has expressed concern that intermediate groups, the secondary associations, should not have aims which are contrary to the 'integrity of the community' so that they may help to 'shore up the larger system of authority with which their own authority is inextricably bound'. Selznick (1952: ch. 7) sees the undermining of an integrated system of values in modern society, and claims the need for a core of shared assumptions on moral values. White (1961: ch. 3) has drawn attention to a whole school of mass society theorists, including such people as David Riesman and William H. Whyte, who may be labelled 'moralisers', because they see the advent of the mass society primarily in the degeneration of values in society. With one final reference to Arnold Rose's statement that the 'nucleus of a voluntary association is a *Gemeinschaft*' (1967: p. 206), the key element of the concern for order among mass society theorists is made explicit in the notion that secondary associations in modern society are a substitute for the order of the organic folk community.

A preoccupation with order and consensus has led to an emphasis on the functions of voluntary associations for social control, explicit in the work of Greer (1958) and Smith (1966); and it is not always made clear that the contribution of associations to the controlling of populations is quite different from their contribution to democracy, though this does emerge from Smith's exposition as he sees the functions of social control for associations to be as applicable in totalitarian as in democratic societies. While it may be that voluntary associations and political parties do contribute to order in society, this should be seen as an empirical question to be dissociated altogether from the theory of mass society. In the first place the postulate that stability, order and consensus are maintained by participation in associations is very weak and unconvincing because the levels of participation are very low for large sectors of the population. More important, and as I hope the preceding exposition has demonstrated, the preoccupation with harmony and order in the theory of mass society is basically antithetical to liberal democratic values: the organic community is the utopia of authoritarian and totalitarian regimes and dictatorships, not of democracies, though it would in fact be quite unfair to label any of the mass society theorists referred to as anti-democratic.

In the empirical analysis of this study no attention has been paid to variables relating to personal adjustment and similar psychological factors because these are not relevant to our concern with social integration and democracy. The equation of personal adjustment with social integration has much in common with the equation of social integration and democracy with harmony and consensus. It is in fact the American political scientists who preach the doctrine of the 'politics of happiness', such as R. E. Lane (1959: ch. 11, and 1965), who have adopted this position, rather than mass society theorists as such.

According to Lane, people who are contented and satisfied citizens are more likely to be active in politics than those who are dissatisfied and alienated. American society is becoming more affluent, people are happier, and the level of consensus on political issues is increasing. The logic of the relationship between happiness and consensus would seem to be that if people are happy they live in harmony with their neighbours, but in view of the trends in American society in recent years, about which some comments will be made in the concluding section here, it is difficult to regard this any longer as of any real significance for American politics. Empirically the relationship between personal adjustment and political participation is a very dubious one: Kornhauser (1960: pp. 90–3) has produced evidence showing that there is no relationship between personal isolation and lack of secondary association ties. A number of studies have assessed the relationship between political apathy and psychological measures of alienation, and much of the evidence is negative. In a study of Columbus, Ohio, Dean (1959–1960) found the correlation between political apathy and alienation so small as to be insignificant, and in a study in Iowa, Erbe (1964) found that a relationship between political apathy and alienation disappeared with various social factors controlled.

Apart from the doubts as to its empirical validity, there are other reasons for questioning the happiness/consensus theory of politics. It suggests that the socially integrated and politically active in society are well-rounded, well-adjusted, good, happy citizens who accept the *status quo*. Now this may conjure up a picture of lots of people harmoniously participating in the activities of lots of overlapping associations, but in view of the predominance of the middle classes in such activities not a very accurate one: what we are left with is a piece of conservative middle-class ideology, as it is implied that people who do not participate in politics and accept things as they are are discontented, anti-social, alienated and anomic,* and, it is tempting to add, people who are not really very nice to know. Alienation and

* *Anomie* here may be taken to mean the state in which individuals are not adequately controlled by norms of behaviour and values.

anomie, taking the meaning of lack of acceptance of the existing state of political society plus value overtones of disapproval, become, as Horton (1964) has argued, ideologically conservative concepts.

It is therefore important to distinguish the theory of mass society from the happiness/consensus theory of politics, and to emphasise that the consideration of social integration and democracy does not at the same time involve any assumptions about personal adjustment. However, it is not the case that the sociological concept of alienation can be dissociated from the theory of mass society, as will be seen shortly. Notwithstanding its ideological connotations, the central thesis of the theory that the decline of the communal society and the rise of industrial society leads to the rise of the mass society unless secondary associations replace the lost communal ties is still valid and useful. The exposure of the ideological roots of a theory does not amount to its refutation, though in his critique of mass society Bramson (1961) appears to assume that it does. From the several characteristics of the abstract conception of the mass society listed by Kornhauser, one of the most important for democratic theory is that social relations among the mass of the population are atomised. This does not mean that everyone is personally disorganised, but that channels of communication between different sectors of the population, and between *élites* and non-*élites* in society are lacking. The mass of the population is alienated from the political process in that most people are not in any meaningful way related to the political process: their reference groups and social perspectives are largely restricted to the isolated small primary groups, such as the family, to which they belong. Social alienation is the opposite of social integration, but not to be equated with psychological feelings of alienation.

The conception of the mass society as a society of atomised and socially alienated masses is important for democratic theory because it postulates that the threat to democracy, or, if one would prefer it, the frustration of democracy, lies in mass apathy rather than in the development of extreme conflicts in society. The theory thus focuses directly on the relationship between political participation and democracy, and as this study has been centred on the consequences of participation, it is important to make explicit here the consequences of its opposite, apathy. First of all, on axiomatic grounds, if a high level of participation in society is a component of democracy, then a society characterised by the predominance of apathy is not democratic. The analysis of the consequences of political participation for democracy in this monograph has proceeded by drawing attention to the differences between people who participate and those who do not, the apathetic, and so the negative consequences of apathy for democracy have been central to the whole argument here. There are, however, more direct ways, according to the theory of mass society, in which apathy threatens democracy, and it is necessary that these should be explained here. Furthermore there is a plausible critique of the theory of mass society to the general effect that a fair degree of political apathy is indicative of the health of a democracy because very high levels of participation indicate the prevalence of extremist, anti-democratic politics and excessive levels of political cleavage. Strange as it may seem, the theory of mass society and its critique here share a number of common assumptions as will emerge from the discussion to follow.

The argument of this monograph has implied that political apathy is an accompaniment of social isolation and alienation; that people who have no connections with intermediate secondary groups in society have a narrow range of social contacts, a narrow social perspective and therefore are unlikely to hold democratic and tolerant attitudes. According to the theory of mass society, the positive danger to democracy lies in that the atomised, apathetic masses are vulnerable to the influence of mass movements which are likely to take anti-democratic forms: the mass society is thus vulnerable to totalitarianism (Kornhauser, 1960: p. 121). The theoretical and empirical basis of this argument is somewhat involved and raises a number of issues which cannot be adequately dealt with in the space of this monograph. It is not, however, a necessary part of the theoretical framework employed here, and only two brief points need be made about it. One of these is that some mass society theorists, such as Ortega y Gasset, are not really talking about threats to democracy but rather threats to the authority of an aristocratic *élite*; and as Bell (1960: p. 28) has shown, these theorists echo an aristocratic fear of 'the masses'. The other point, a constructive rather than critical one, is that the theory does suggest that if sizeable groups in society are not in any way related to the communication channels of the political process, then if they do become aroused to demand the exercise of power and influence, this will be through direct, uncompromising and often violent means. This may appear as no more than a rewording of the notion that alienated and atomised populations provide fruitful recruiting grounds for extremist mass movements, but does in fact represent a substantial revision. The substance of the revision is to shift the focus of the theory from the 'condition of the masses', with its aristocratic connotations, to the structure of society. Political apathy on a large scale indicates that sizeable groups in society are alienated from the political process and thus excluded from the communication channels of the political process. Such groups have no other recourse to power and influence than direct, uninstitutionalised means: and because they are socially isolated their demands are likely to be intolerant, uncompromising and thus anti-democratic. Even if it is the case that such groups remain apathetic and content to be excluded from the political process, society is more orderly but hardly more democratic.

The critique of the theory of mass society in the defence of apathy takes two major forms, the first stemming from political theory and the second from political sociology, but only the first is convincing. The argument of Morris Jones (1954) that notions of the duty to vote and enforced participation are more appropriate to totalitarian than liberal democracy is sound and useful. A democratic society is a tolerant society, and one of the things it should tolerate is political apathy. This does not in fact detract from our argument as to the importance of participation, but serves as a reminder that even if participation is a component of democracy, society is not made more democratic by forcing everyone at gun-point, to use an extreme example, to participate. Morris Jones has also argued against a conception of democracy according to which the extent of democracy is measurable according to the level of participation in favour of one according to which democracy ensures the expression and clash of interests in society. It may, however, be argued that the expression and clash of interests at every level in society depends on a minimal level of participation at each level. The reason for treating voluntary association participation as political participation in this study is that voluntary associations are vehicles for the articulation of interests, that they are pressure groups with at least the potential for exercising influence in society. At the same time the inadequacy of levels of participation alone as a measure of democracy is clearly demonstrable: a high level of participation which is predominantly middle class might indicate the dominance of middle-class interests and the exclusion of others from the political forum, whereas lower levels of participation more evenly balanced between different social sectors would indicate a wider representation of interests in the political process.

The theoretical defence of apathy discussed above is useful in showing the weaknesses of the naïve assumption of a one-to-one relationship between political participation and democracy. It is not incompatible with the theoretical approach adopted here because it need not involve the notion that apathy as such makes a positive contribution to democracy. This notion, which can be broadly regarded as a product of political sociology rather than political theory, is now subjected to critical examination. The core of the argument is that a fair measure of apathy indicates the stability of democracy and high levels of consensus, that people are generally satisfied with the way political affairs are conducted. As Lipset (1960: p. 32) has put it, echoing the views of a number of political scientists and sociologists, 'an increase in the level of participation may reflect the *decline* of social cohesion and the breakdown of the democratic process; whereas a stable democracy may rest on the general belief that the outcome of an election will not make too great a difference in society'. There are two distinct elements to this reasoning. The first rests on the assumption that democracy depends upon order and consensus, and that high levels of participation indicate the intensification of conflict and cleavage in society and thus

124 The Sociology of Grass Roots Politics

threaten the democratic order: as the equation of democracy with order and consensus has been rejected, this need not be discussed further here. The second element rests on the evidence that the politically apathetic are likely to be intolerant, authoritarian and opposed to democratic values, evidence which has been employed to advance the argument of this monograph, and also utilises the contribution of the happiness/consensus theory of politics to the effect that the apathetic are discontented, alienated and anomic. McClosky (1964), in a study showing a low level of consensus on liberal-democratic values among the politically apathetic, has argued that the apathetic do not threaten democratic institutions because of their apathy: it follows that if such people who are normally apathetic become politically active, their activity will take anti-democratic forms. This does share common ground with certain aspects of the theory of mass society, but differs from our postulate that those excluded from the communication channels of the political process will seek power and influence by direct and uninstitutionalised means, in that it locates the characteristics of the apathetic in the 'condition of the masses' rather than the structure of society. Illustration of this fear of the masses is provided by Lipset's (1960: ch. 4) thesis that the working-class culture and way of life is conducive to authoritarianism, a proposition shown by Miller and Riessman (1961) and Lipsitz (1965) to be of dubious empirical validity. What is implied by the thesis is that perhaps it is rather a good thing that working-class political participation is low, because the working class are anti-democratic. To come to the point, the justification of apathy in terms of the characteristics of the apathetic masses turns out to be a piece of ideological sophistry: people who are politically apathetic do not have the same democratic attitudes as people who do participate, and therefore it is best that they should remain apathetic. If the view is accepted that political participation in itself fosters democratic attitudes, then it is rather like saying that people who have never driven a motor-car should never be allowed to drive one because they do not know how. This represents something of an oversimplification, however, because while the concern with political participation here

Theory and Problems of Grass Roots Politics 125

has been in terms of secondary association links, Lipset and others of his persuasion are really talking only about voting, and it is quite reasonable to argue that if those who are apathetic and alienated from the political process do vote, they are likely to respond to anti-democratic appeals. The frequently cited demonstration of this is the high electoral turnout in Germany in the 1930s, which is sufficient proof for the proposition that a high electoral turnout is not indicative of the strength of democracy. But this is not evidence for the converse, that a low electoral turnout indicates the strength of democracy: electoral turnout in the 1936 election in Japan was low (Barrington Moore, 1967: p. 300). The more appropriate conclusion is that voting in itself does not provide much indication of the strength or weakness of democratic processes, and that a proper consideration of the consequences of political participation for democracy requires the examination of forms of participation other than voting, which is, of course, what has been attempted here.

The discussion of apathy here has proved rather lengthy, but cannot be concluded without some mention of the thesis, advanced by Etzioni (1961: p. 24), that low levels of participation are functional for the efficiency of most political parties and voluntary associations. It is probably the case that most political parties and voluntary associations possess predominantly apathetic memberships, and that the structure and organisation of such associations is geared to this apathy: it would therefore follow that a large upsurge in participation would render the existing structure of such organisations unworkable. Increased participation therefore may well be dysfunctional for the *status quo* of such associations, but this is neither profound nor enlightening. There are no *a priori* grounds for assuming that the structure of an organisation is not amenable to change in order to cope with increased levels of participation: indeed, if the author's view is taken that the conception of social structure derives from the way groups of people behave in society rather than rigid, static entities such as 'the organisation', then a sharp increase in participation may in itself amount to the change of the structure of an association. The argument here is rather abstract and condensed, but the structure and organisation of political parties and associations is a subject beyond the scope of the present analysis. Sufficient has been said, it is hoped, to show that the case for the functions of apathy for organisational efficiency is not a valid defence of apathy.

The final issue to be considered in this theoretical reassessment is the threat of extremist politics to democratic systems, and unlike most of the previously discussed issues there is much agreement on this among both exponents and critics of the theory of mass society. Mass society theorists see the dangers of extremism in political alienation and apathy, whereas their critics see no dangers in apathy as such, but both are agreed that the threat to democracy lies in extremist politics. The label of extremism is not, however, a very precise one for political analysis, and carries value overtones of disapproval. To render the notion useful, it is necessary to distinguish two separate aspects of the postulate that extremist politics threaten democracy. The first rests on the assumption that democratic politics depend on order and consensus, and it need hardly be added that this will be rejected here: extremist politics are politics which do not accept the legitimacy of the democratic order, that conflicts in society should be contained within an overriding consensus as to the legitimacy of the basic political institutions in society. In the first place, this definition of extremism is ideological and of no general validity in that it defines extremism in relation to the prevailing ideology of the ruling groups in a particular society, rather than in terms of democratic principles. More important, in the last analysis it is not compatible with democratic principles. As Dahrendorf has put it, democratic politics are the politics of uncertainty:

> We are assuming that nobody knows or can know what form of social order is ultimately satisfactory, good, just. If this is the case, it follows that the bad society, the clearly unjust society, can be avoided only if and so long as the conflict between different conceptions of the just society is kept alive. Uncertainty requires competition, social and political conflict, and institutions that provide suitable conditions for this conflict. (1968b: p. 247)

Theory and Problems of Grass Roots Politics 127

Democracy proceeds by trial and error, and the clash of interests and opinions, and would seem to negate itself if it demands unquestioning belief in the infallibility of current institutional arrangements. Without becoming too involved in questions that are more appropriately answered by political theorists than sociologists, it may be asserted that democratic, moderate politics are maintained not by an imposed consensus but by the flow of communications, the social interaction between different political groups in society: such interaction necessarily involves common acceptance of procedures for channelling political discussion and conflict, but no overriding consensus. It follows that politics which are outside the interaction and communication network of the political process in society are likely to be extremist politics.

The second approach to extremism is therefore in terms of isolation from political institutions rather than lack of consensus as to their legitimacy. Extremist political organisations are those which are isolated at all levels from the political process, and at the grass roots level this occurs partly through social ostracism, but more especially in terms of our theoretical approach, because the organisations demand total commitment and attempt to dominate their members. Kornhauser (1962) has documented an empirical study showing how the total commitment of certain radical groups in Chicago involves their complete social isolation. Extremist politics are therefore to be defined in terms of the total commitment they demand and the control they seek to exercise over their members. As has been argued in the theoretical approach here, only political participation in associations which are characterised by partial levels of control and commitment is conducive to social integration and democracy.

The purpose of this rather lengthy section has been to substantiate our claim, made in Chapter 1, regarding the relevance of the theory of mass society for the understanding of grass roots politics in Britain. The starting-point here has been the refutation of the notions that the theory is either not applicable to class-based politics or else applicable only to middle-class politics. This has been shown to involve dissociating the theory from statements as to the consequences of political participation

128 The Sociology of Grass Roots Politics

for order, consensus and personal adjustment. It has followed that objections to the theory on the grounds that a measure of apathy is conducive to democracy are untenable, although assessment of the defence of apathy has been fruitful in showing that, notwithstanding the consequences of political participation for social integration and democracy in terms of the theory, it is quite wrong to use participation as a sole measure of democracy. From the postulates of the theory of mass society that the politically apathetic are likely to be politically alienated, and that the politically alienated are likely to be extremist in political action, this has led finally to a short consideration of the dangers of extremist politics to democratic processes: these dangers have been seen to lie in the exclusion, voluntary or otherwise, of extremist groups from the communication channels of the political process, and not in their possession of ideologies which do not accept a supra-party consensus as to the legitimacy of prevailing political institutions. This refocuses on the central argument of this monograph, which the empirical analysis has gone some way to demonstrate, that it is only political participation in limited secondary associations, with memberships that are heterogeneous and cross-cutting to allow the spread of social contacts and communication channels, which contributes to social integration and democracy.

The exposition of the theoretical framework in the first chapter of this monograph necessarily left several issues unsatisfactorily resolved, and if in this chapter some of these have been settled, others have emerged to replace them. The theory of mass society has a long and rich intellectual history, and though some attention has been paid to its ideological background and implications, the exposition here has been confined to those aspects of the theory that are relevant to a consideration of the relationship between political participation, social integration and democracy.

Grass Roots Participation and Contemporary Politics

If the theory of mass society does further an understanding of the place of grass roots politics in Britain, then it is only fitting in conclusion to give some indication of its application to the contemporary political scene. The argument in the preceding section has been largely at a somewhat abstract level, and in this concluding section some attempt is made to draw out some of the implications for practical politics from what might otherwise appear to be the rather arid produce of an ivory tower.

To begin with fundamentals, the theoretical approach adopted here implies the rejection of two classically opposed approaches to the understanding of political participation in Britain. The first of these is the Marxian notion that the political process is to be understood in terms of the internecine class struggle, and little need be said about this here. The empirical analysis of political participation above has stressed the importance of the channelling of class interests in the political process and the distribution of participation through different social strata; but as Aron (1968: p. 20) has argued, the conflicts and disagreements among different social groups in industrial society, to which our analysis has referred, are in no way to be equated with the Marxian class struggle: it is Aron's suggestion that this equation is a product of Marxist–Leninist ideology, and there is no need to take issue with this here.

The opposite approach is to see the operation of an overwhelming consensus as to the legitimacy of current political arrangements as central to the understanding of the British political process. The elements of this approach are explicit in a paper by Rothman (1961). The development of the modern British political system has, according to the argument, been one of gradual and moderate reform, contained within an attachment to the national community. 'Britain entered upon modernity as a *Gemeinschaft* . . . a collectivity whose members are bound together by affective ties to the collectivity itself, and to each other as members of the collectivity.' Parliament is accepted as 'a body searching to discover and implement the general will of the community', and the monarchy is a symbol of unity representing the organic community. Apart from the fact that the language of *Gemeinschaft*, organic community and Rousseau's general will are more appropriate for authoritarian and totalitarian regimes than democracies, the doctrine of gradualism expounded by Rothman is very much open to question. Barrington Moore's (1967: ch. 1) analysis has shown the extensive violence underlying the apparent gradualist progress of England towards democracy. On the other hand, it should be made clear that the rejection of the consensus approach does not involve any denial of the existence of levels of consensus in British politics. For example, there is no intention of questioning the existence of widespread consensus on the place of the monarchy, which has been claimed by Shils & Young (1953) and denied ideologically and unconvincingly by Birnbaum (1955). The point here is rather to question whether such consensus is really very important in understanding the British political process.

If the key to the democratic political process is a national community consensus, it must follow that the Scottish and Welsh Nationalist parties, which do not accept the legitimacy of the prevailing political system, are a threat to democratic processes, which is an absurd proposition. It is much more plausible to argue that these parties contribute to rather than detract from democratic processes. Even if they do not approve of it, they do work through the existing communication channels of the political process. They are partial and limited in terms of control and commitment, and it would seem likely that their memberships are at least as heterogeneous and subject to cross-cutting ties as those of the Labour and Conservative parties. It is worth adding that support for the nationalist parties represents to some degree the concern for a greater spread of participation and influence in decision-making, and less centralised control. There is no reason why political participation in parties not accepting the consensus regarding current political arrangements should not contribute to social integration and democracy, though it is not unlikely that such groups, if they maintain popular support but fail to secure any effective influence on political events, will have recourse to extremism, with its consequent direct and violent methods of political action.

Apart from the rise of nationalist parties, however, British politics in the late 1960s would appear to be characterised by increasingly higher levels of consensus. In fact, the development of what has now become popularly known as consensus politics

Theory and Problems of Grass Roots Politics 131

may be viewed as a matter for concern rather than complacency or satisfaction. This, it may be admitted, is also the view of certain politicians of the rather extreme right, such as Mr Enoch Powell, and also of the rather extreme left, such as elements of the Young Liberals, and not that of the happiness/consensus school of political science. Here the concern is solely with negative consequences of consensus for grass roots politics, which are really twofold.

The first, already alluded to in Chapter 4 (p. 88), is that consensus is conducive to political apathy. If there are no important differences and conflicts apparent between the parties, political participation declines. As Kornhauser (1962) has shown in his study of Chicago, the problem for liberal parties is one of maintaining the commitment and interest of the members when the disparity between political expectations and achievements is so small as to give little incentive for political action. It is hardly necessary to repeat that the level of party political participation of party members found in this and other British studies is very low. The really interesting question is whether in fact grass roots political participation in Britain is increasing or declining, but it is one to which no satisfactory answer is possible. According to official party figures, the nationalist parties possessed larger memberships than other parties in Scotland and Wales in 1968, and as this rise is recent and does not appear to be accompanied by a collapse in grass roots participation in any of the established parties, it would seem to be the case that grass roots participation is increasing in Scotland and Wales, though this is little more than speculation. In England, what little evidence there is points to a decline rather than an increase in participation. A recent study of the Labour Party in Liverpool has shown a decline in party membership, and national party membership figures do show some decline in recent years, but in view of the grossness of these figures, the change is small enough to be explicable in terms of either an improvement or a decline in the efficiency of keeping party records. There is certainly, however, no evidence of any increase in political participation in England. If it is difficult enough to assess trends in party membership, it is quite impossible to make any generalisations about trends in voluntary association participation in Britain, which has also been treated here as a form of political participation.

The second, and perhaps more significant, negative consequence of consensus for grass roots politics rests on the very reasonable assumption that consensus among political parties and influential interest groups does not necessarily reflect the same consensus among the general population. The consensus may in fact simply reflect the suppression of conflict, the exclusion of groups not accepting the consensus from the political process, or at least the failure of the political process to channel interest which might conflict with the consensus. At the grass roots level this may be closely connected with the consequences of consensus for apathy: people may be apathetic because as the parties are seen as no different from one another, then no party is seen as supporting their particular interests. The United States probably reflects the achievement of consensus by the exclusion of certain interest groups from the political process more clearly than Britain. Consensus among the 1968 presidential election candidates – all, for example, stressed the importance of law and order – could be seen as denying any channel for the expression of liberal and social reform interests. The happiness/consensus theory of politics must surely depend for its empirical verification on evidence from samples restricted to white occupants of northern cities. If the picture is less pronounced in Britain than in America, it is still to some extent the case that here the politics of consensus excludes certain interests and opinions from the political process. Student disturbances, as forms of extremist political behaviour, may be regarded as a consequence of the exclusion of students as an interest group from effective participation in institutionalised political processes: this exclusion may be seen as stemming from the paternalistic and authoritarian structures of the institutions of higher education. As a somewhat more important example, it is questionable how far the interests of retired persons, people characterised by high levels of political apathy, are influential in the political process. Wilensky (1961) has suggested that the increasing social isolation of old people may render

Theory and Problems of Grass Roots Politics 133

them susceptible to the influence of extremist politics. These examples are speculative and subject to considerable empirical qualification, but they suffice to illustrate the point that consensus politics may mean that significant conflicts in society are neither assimilated nor regulated but suppressed: the consequences may be apathy or ultimately direct and violent political action.

The practical conclusion often drawn from studies of political and voluntary association participation is that more people should be encouraged to participate in community affairs; but the analysis here suggests that this conclusion needs substantial modification. In the first place, a simple aggregate increase in participation may well be concentrated among those groups for whom participation is already fairly high, and this would serve only to strengthen these groups already exercising disproportionate influence. As Lapping (1968: p. 186) has noted, local associations set up to protect local interests such as those of consumers might function to serve middle-class interests and thus enhance class differences. The second qualification is that the spread of participation requires a balanced range of associations so that there are not groups of people who do not participate either because they do not find associations reflecting their interests or because they feel that in certain associations they will be excluded from any effective influence. These qualifications in no way detract from the importance of participation for the working of democracy.

Apart from voting, the question of participation has never been a very prominent one for British politicians and political scientists. As Barker (ed. Lapping & Radice, 1968: p. 18) has noted, within the Labour Party this issue has been very much overshadowed by concern with economic inequalities. As Radice has remarked in another paper in the same Fabian publication (ed. Lapping & Radice, 1968: p. 5), 'The truth is that democracy, for British Socialists, has been a second order problem, taken for granted as part of the political scenery. Labour supporters believed that the election of a Labour government would, in itself, be a significant strengthening of democracy.' It would be unfair to conclude with this quotation if it was applicable only to the Labour Party.

Appendix Theory, Methodology and Statistics

The theory of mass society as developed in this monograph presupposes an interactionist approach to sociology, and the statistical procedures employed here, those of rank correlation and the test factor standardisation method of partial correlation, are ones which are compatible with this approach, whereas more fashionable techniques, such as the use of tests of significance, are not. To explain the relationship between empirical theory, meta-theoretical approach and empirical methodology would take up the best part of a further monograph. Here no more can be done than to point briefly to a few of the more fundamental issues involved: this is followed by explanations of the empirical procedures employed.

Central to the theory of mass society developed here is the postulate concerning the consequences of social relationships and social interaction for the individual's perspective and view of the world and for the structure of society. The interactionist approach to sociology involves viewing society as an on-going social process, as composed of a complex web of social relationships and social interaction, and not as an abstract social structure reducible to numbers of static variables which socially determine the behaviour of individuals. Thus some interactionist sociologists, such as Blumer (1962), reject the statistical analysis of variables as an approach to sociological investigation. This is an unnecessary step if variables are regarded not as abstract entities affecting individuals, but as abstractions of on-going interaction processes. The variables analysed in this monograph, such as association membership and participation, exposure to communications, and the *expression* of attitudes, mostly refer directly to social interaction. Even variables of social class and stratification, in that they refer to the occupancy of roles within and identification with particular social groups, may similarly be regarded as referring ultimately to processes of social interaction. The theory of mass society implies that the effects of such variables are the consequences of the dynamics of social interaction: the consequences of political participation follow directly from participation itself, rather than from any resulting exposure of the participants to new external societal pressures or social determinants.

What this means for statistical analysis is that certain techniques, such as those of tests of significance, are inappropriate because they involve making untenable assumptions about human populations. Tests of significance were developed for biological and agricultural research before being adopted by sociologists, and the validity of this adoption is questioned by the interactionist approach. It is inappropriate to apply the same statistical techniques to both fields of corn and human populations, because it may be assumed that ears of wheat do not interact with one another whereas human populations do. There are in fact other, more specific, arguments to the effect that significance tests are often inappropriate for sociological analysis, as shown so well by Selvin (1957). Unless all uncontrolled variables are randomised, and clearly this is not possible, correlated biases may exceed random errors, in which case tests of significance are meaningless: in any case the meaning of significance tests is essentially negative, for levels of significance may be interpreted solely as the probability of rejecting the null hypothesis that there is no difference between two populations when it is actually true, but appears false because of random accidents; which does not add up to very much. There is no real basis for theoretical distinctions between differences that have a 1 per cent chance of occurring through random error and those with a 0·1 per cent chance. Anyway, statistically significant differences may be theoretically insignificant, and the converse also applies.

The statistical measures of association selected for analysis here are thus descriptive measures, which do not in themselves permit statistical inference from samples to the universe. Their value lies in the provision of meaningful, quantitative descriptions of the attributes of the samples, which could not anyway be shown by significance tests. In that the concern here has been with the empirical illustration of theoretical propositions rather

Theory, Methodology and Statistics 137

than simple empirical generalisations, generalisation does not depend upon any necessary statistical inference from the samples to the universe. It may, however, be added that most of the important correlations analysed here refer to differences which would indicate a normally acceptable level of statistical significance; and that these are not a random collection of correlations, but ones which are theoretically consistent, would strengthen the case for statistical significance: but this is not directly relevant to our methodology.

The measure most frequently employed in this study is that of γ developed by Goodman & Kruskal (1954). This is a symmetric measure of association for ordinal variables, with a value varying between -1, 0 and $+1$. Any given value of γ may be interpreted as the difference between the conditional probabilities of like and unlike order, under the condition that ties on both dependent and independent variables are ignored. The computation is very simple, and illustration of this is given for a 2×3 table, but is very similar for tables with any number of cells:

	X_1	X_2
Y_1	a	b
Y_2	c	d
Y_3	e	f

$$\gamma = \frac{P-Q}{P+Q}$$

where $P = a(d+f) + cf$ (concordant pairs)
and $Q = b(c+e) + de$ (discordant pairs)

Thus:

Opinion Leadership and Association Activity

	Activists	*Non-participants*
Rated leaders on two questions	15	5
Rated leaders on one question	21	23
Not rated on either question	18	83
	54	111

$$P = 15 \times (23+83) + 21 \times 83 = 3333$$
$$Q = 5 \times (21+18) + 23 \times 18 = 609$$
$$P+Q = 3942$$
$$P-Q = 2724$$
$$\therefore \gamma = \frac{2724}{3942} = 0.691$$

expressing the probability that people who are active in voluntary associations are more likely to be opinion leaders than those who are inactive.

Because this measure avoids ties on both variables, its use is not always appropriate when there are large numbers of ties, as very small differences between categories may produce very large correlation coefficients: thus a different coefficient, Somers's d (Somers, 1962) has sometimes been employed in the analysis. This is also a measure of association for ordinal variables, with values ranging between -1, 0 and $+1$. It has a similar interpretation to γ, except that in this case, ties on the dependent variable are taken into account. The value of d thus expresses the proportionate excess of concordant over discordant pairs not tied on the independent variable, or, alternatively, the difference between the conditional probabilities of like and unlike order, under the condition that ties on the independent variable are ignored. Unlike the statistic γ, this coefficient is asymmetric and requires a distinction between the dependent and independent variables. For analysis of the relationship between two variables, it is necessary to make the procedural assumption of designating one of these as independent and the other as dependent. This does impose certain restrictions on its application, which is why the coefficient d has been employed fairly sparsely. In the first place, because the incidence of party membership among the people interviewed in Walton was determined by the sampling technique, it is not permissible to treat party membership as a dependent variable. There would be no point in taking ties on the variable of party membership into account when these are solely a product of the sampling design. On the other hand, the procedural assumption that party membership is the independent variable is not valid unless party membership may be assumed to be at least in part antecedent to the other variable: for example, it would be absurd to regard type of schooling as in any way dependent upon party membership. It is worth emphasising that the procedural assumption of dependence and independence of variables is not an empirical assumption concerning the direction of causality – the statistic d is employed here solely for correlation and not for any causal analysis – but it is nevertheless logically invalid to treat an empirically antecedent variable as dependent.

As the coefficient d is asymmetric, it has two forms, according to which variable is assumed to be independent: d_{yx} where x is the independent variable and d_{xy} where y is the independent variable. Only one form has been employed in the analysis here, treating party membership as the independent variable, and age, sex, education and social class as independent variables in relation to authoritarian attitudes.

For illustration, the computation of the two forms of the coefficient from a 2×3 table is given, though the computation is similar for tables with any number of cells. As stated above, the coefficient d differs from γ in that ties on the dependent variable are taken into account. Thus, taking x as the dependent variable,

	X_1	X_2	
Y_1	a	b	B_1
Y_2	c	d	B_2
Y_3	e	f	B_3
	A_1	A_2	

$$d_{xy} = \frac{P-Q}{P+Q+X_0}$$

Similarly, taking y as the dependent variable,

$$d_{yx} = \frac{P-Q}{P+Q+Y_0}$$

where $P = a(d+f)+cf$ (number of concordant pairs)
$Q = b(c+e)+de$ (number of discordant pairs)
$X_0 = a(c+e)+ce+b(d+f)+df$ (number of pairs tied on x only)
$Y_0 = ab+cd+ef$ (number of pairs tied on y only)

For computation,
let
$$P+Q+Y_0 = X_u$$
and
$$P+Q+X_0 = Y_u$$

Then, for the given 2×3 table, it may be calculated that
$$Y_u = B_1 B_2 + B_1 B_3 + B_2 B_3$$
$$X_u = A_1 A_2$$

Therefore,
$$d_{xy} = \frac{P-Q}{B_1B_2+B_1B_3+B_2B_3}$$
$$d_{yx} = \frac{P-Q}{A_1A_2}$$

Thus:

Education and Authoritarian Attitudes

	Authoritarian scale score		
Type of school attended	Low	High	Total
1. Independent or grammar	13	8	21
2. Technical or central	10	5	15
3. Secondary modern or elementary	39	95	134
	62	108	170

Education (Y) is taken as the independent variable, and authoritarian attitudes (X) as the dependent variable, and thus the coefficient d_{xy} is employed for analysis.

$$P = 13 \times (5+95) + 10 \times 95 = 2250$$
$$Q = 8 \times (10+39) + 5 \times 39 = 587$$
$$P+Q+X_0 = Y_u = 21 \times 15 + 21 \times 134 + 15 \times 134 = 5139$$
$$P-Q = 2250 - 587 = 1663$$

$$\therefore d_{xy} = \frac{1663}{5139} = 0.324$$

expressing the probability that the higher the category of schooling, the less likely is the individual to express authoritarian attitudes, taking into account ties on the variable of schooling.

Theory, Methodology and Statistics 141

The method of test factor standardisation, in which both the above described coefficients are employed in this study, was introduced to sociological research by Rosenberg (1962-3). This technique enables the relationship between two variables to be analysed when the effect of a third variable, the test factor, is controlled or standardised. For illustration, let the two variables to be analysed be X and Y, and the test factor to be controlled be q. The initial table showing the relationship between X and Y ignores the variable q.

	X_1	X_2	X_3
Y_1	a	b	c
Y_2	d	e	f
Y_3	g	h	i

From this table, for each value of the variable q that is being taken into account a separate table is compiled. If the two variables for analysis were social class and authoritarian attitudes, and the test factor was education, then a separate table is prepared for the respondents in each educational category. Thus:

q_1				q_2				q_3			
	X_1	X_2	X_3		X_1	X_2	X_3		X_1	X_2	X_3
Y_1	a_1	b_1	c_1	Y_1	a_2	b_2	c_2	Y_1	a_3	b_3	c_3
Y_2	d_1	e_1	f_1	Y_2	d_2	e_2	f_2	Y_2	d_3	e_3	f_3
Y_3	g_1	h_1	i_1	Y_3	g_2	h_2	i_2	Y_3	g_3	h_3	i_3

For each test factor category, the number, or proportion, in each cell is multiplied by the proportion in each q category. If the category q_1 – perhaps for the analysis of social class and authoritarianism representing those with the minimal years of schooling – contains 55 per cent of the total sample, then each cell in the table for q_1 is multiplied by 0·55. With this step completed, the corresponding cells for each q category (a_1, a_2, a_3, etc.) are then summarised to produce a new table for the variables X and Y, with the factor q standardised.

142 The Sociology of Grass Roots Politics

It is possible, using this procedure, to standardise by several variables simultaneously. Supposing that in addition to the q factor, the factor v is also to be controlled, then, following the procedure set out above, every table for each category of q must now be broken down into separate tables for each level of v. If, in addition to standardising the relationship between social class and authoritarian attitudes by education, standardisation is required for rural/urban differences, then each educational category must be broken down into rural and urban categories, and a separate table prepared for each. Thus:

$$q_1$$

	v_1				v_2		
	X_1	X_2	X_3		X_1	X_2	X_3
Y_1	a_{11}	b_{11}	c_{11}	Y_1	a_{12}	b_{12}	c_{12}
Y_2	d_{11}	e_{11}	f_{11}	Y_2	d_{12}	e_{12}	f_{12}
Y_3	g_{11}	h_{11}	i_{11}	Y_3	g_{12}	h_{12}	i_{12}

If there are three levels of the factor q, and two levels of the factor v, then for standardisation by the two factors simultaneously, there will be six test factor categories, and for each of these categories the number or proportion in each cell is multiplied by the proportion in the vq category. Suppose, in standardising social class and authoritarian attitudes by education and rural/urban residence, 20 per cent of the total sample reside in rural areas and have the minimal schooling, represented in the category q_1v_1: then each cell for the table q_1v_1 is multiplied by 0·20. The corresponding cells in each vq category (a_{11}, a_{12}, a_{21}, a_{22}, etc.) are then summarised to produce a new table for the variables X and Y, with the factors v and q standardised. It is possible to standardise by further variables at the same time, though there is the limitation that each cell in every category must contain at least one case. In this study, standardisation has not been carried out for more than two variables simultaneously. Our interest is not, of course, in the standardised distributions as such emerging from this analysis, but rather in

Theory, Methodology and Statistics 143

the difference between the standardised and unstandardised distributions, which is demonstrated in the text by comparison of the respective rank correlation coefficients.

According to Rosenberg (1962-3), the chief interest of test factor standardisation is the extent to which relationships may be reduced, perhaps even eliminated, and thus causally explained, by the control of test factors. However, the employment of test factor standardisation and other techniques of partial correlation for causal analysis has been shown by Arnold Rose (1954: ch. 17) to be methodologically unsound in most social research. Here the technique has been employed solely for descriptive purposes, and has been found useful in describing the relationships between sets of variables. The analysis has been as interesting for relationships between variables which have been increased by the control of test factors as for reduced relationships. Indeed, for descriptive purposes the technique is methodologically stronger when it produces increased rather than reduced relationships. This is because of the tendency for standardisation of the test factor to result in the partial standardisation of one of the variables under analysis, particularly where there is a strong relationship between the variable and the test factor: thus any reduction of the relationship may be due to this partial standardisation of one of the variables rather than the test factor, and it is not possible to assess how far this is the case. This problem does not arise where the standardisation results in increased relationships. Increased relationships resulting from partial correlations are rarely reported in the literature, though a high proportion of the partial correlations undertaken in this study have resulted in increased rather than reduced relationships.

Increased relationships normally occur where the standardising factor is related in different ways to the two variables under analysis. Thus the correlation coefficient showing Conservative Party members to be more active in associations than the electors is increased when the proportions of the sexes are standardised (Table 3:7, p. 59). This is because there is a much higher proportion of women in the Conservative group, but at the same time women are less likely to be active in associations than men.

However, increased relationships can also occur where the standardising factor is related in the same way to both variables. Thus, the correlation coefficient showing Conservative Party members to be more active in associations than the electors is also increased when occupational class is standardised (Table 4:2, p. 71). The Conservative group contains a higher proportion of middle-class people than the group of electors, and there is overall evidence from Walton, consistent with previous studies, that middle-class people are more likely to be active in associations than working-class people. The unexpected increased relationship occurs here because, contrary to the general pattern, among the Conservatives in Walton it is the working-class members who are the more active in associations (pp. 70-1). The methodological significance of such a finding for interactionist sociology is considerable. Social class is not a mechanistic variable operating upon individuals independently of social interaction, but refers to the interaction of individuals in their role relationships in social groups, and the effects of this interaction may be changed if other interaction variables (in this instance membership of the Conservative Party) intervene. Some insight into interaction processes may therefore be gained through the application of the technique of standardisation to variable analysis.

Bibliography

This bibliography should not be regarded as in any sense exhaustive or inclusive: only works cited or referred to in the text are listed.

Abrams, Philip, and Little, Alan, 'The Young Activist in British Politics', in *British Journal of Sociology*, xvi (1965) 315-33.
Adorno, T. W., et al., *The Authoritarian Personality* (New York: Harper, 1950).
Agger, Robert E., and Ostrom, Vincent, 'Political Participation in a Small Community', in *Political Behaviour*, ed. H. Eulau et al. (New York: Free Press of Glencoe, 1956).
Allardt, Erik, et al., 'On the Cumulative Nature of Leisure Activities', in *Acta Sociologica*, III (1958) 165-72.
Allardt, Erik, and Pesonen, Pertti, 'Citizen Participation in Political Life: Finland', in *International Social Science Journal*, XII (1960) 27-39.
Allardt, Erik, 'Community Activity, Leisure Use and Social Structure', in *Acta Sociologica*, VI (1962) 67-82.
Allardt, Erik, 'Patterns of Class Conflict and Working Class Consciousness in Finnish Politics', in *Cleavages, Ideologies and Party Systems*, ed. E. Allardt and Y. Littunen (Helsinki: Westermarck Society, 1964).
Almond, G. A., and Verba, Sidney, *The Civic Culture: political attitudes and democracy in five nations* (Princeton: Princeton University Press, 1963).
Anderson, Bo, et al., 'On Conservative Attitudes', in *Acta Sociologica*, VIII (1965) 189-203.
Arendt, Hannah, *The Origins of Totalitarianism*, 2nd ed. (London: Allen & Unwin, 1958).
Aron, Raymond, *Progress and Disillusion: the dialectics of modern society* (London: Pall Mall, 1968).
Barnes, Samuel H., *Party Democracy: politics in an Italian socialist federation* (London: Yale University Press, 1967).
Bealey, Frank, et al., *Constituency Politics: a study of electoral behaviour in Newcastle-under-Lyme* (London: Faber, 1965).
Bell, Daniel, *The End of Ideology: on the exhaustion of political ideas in the fifties* (New York: Free Press of Glencoe, 1960).
Bell, Wendell, and Force, Maryanne T., 'Urban Neighbourhood Types and Participation in Formal Organisations', in *American Sociological Review*, XXI (1956) 25-34.
Bell, Wendell, and Boat, Marion D., 'Urban Neighbourhoods and Informal Social Relations', in *American Journal of Sociology*, LXII (1956-7) 391-8.
Benney, Mark, et al., *How People Vote: a study of electoral behaviour in Greenwich* (London: Routledge & Kegan Paul, 1956).

Berry, David, 'The Significance of Party Membership: Rank and File Members in a Liverpool Constituency' (M.A. thesis, University of Liverpool, 1967).
Berry, David, 'Party Membership and Social Participation', in *Political Studies*, XVII (1969) 196–207.
Bettelheim, Bruno, and Janowitz, Morris, *Social Change and Prejudice* (New York: Free Press of Glencoe, 1964).
Birch, A. H., *Small Town Politics* (Oxford: O.U.P., 1959).
Birnbaum, Norman, 'Monarchs and Sociologists: a reply to Professor Shils and Mr Young', in *Sociological Review*, III (1955) 5–23.
Blondel, J., *Voters, Parties and Leaders: the social fabric of British politics* (Harmondsworth: Penguin Books, 1963).
Blumer, Herbert, 'Society as Symbolic Interaction', in *Human Behaviour and Social Processes: an interactionist approach*, ed. Arnold M. Rose (London: Routledge & Kegan Paul, 1962).
Bott, Elizabeth, 'The Concept of Class as a Reference Group', in *Human Relations*, VII (1954) 259–83.
Bottomore, T. B., 'Social Stratification in Voluntary Organisations', in *Social Mobility in Britain*, ed. David Glass (London: Routledge & Kegan Paul, 1954).
Bracey, H. E., *Neighbours: on new estates and subdivisions in England and the U.S.A.* (London: Routledge & Kegan Paul, 1964).
Bramson, Leon, *The Political Context of Sociology* (Princeton: Princeton University Press, 1961).
Campbell, Angus, et al., *The Voter Decides* (Evanston: Row, Peterson, 1954).
Campbell, Angus, 'The Passive Citizen', in *Acta Sociologica*, VI (1962) 9–27.
Carter, Roy E. Jnr, and Clarke, Peter, 'Opinion Leadership among Educational Television Viewers', in *American Sociological Review*, XXVII (1962) 792–9.
Cauter, T., and Downham, J. S., *The Communication of Ideas: a study of contemporary influences on urban life* (London: Readers' Digest Association, 1954).
Centers, Richard, *The Psychology of Social Classes* (Princeton: Princeton University Press, 1949).
Chapman, Dennis, *Home and Social Status* (London: Routledge & Kegan Paul, 1955).
Curtis, Richard F., et al., 'Prejudice and Urban Social Participation', in *American Journal of Sociology*, LXXIII (1967–8) 235–44.
Dahl, Robert A., *Who Governs? Democracy and power in an American city* (New Haven: Yale University Press, 1961).
Dahrendorf, Ralf, *Class and Class Conflict in Industrial Society* (London: Routledge & Kegan Paul, 1959).
Dahrendorf, Ralf, *Society and Democracy in Germany* (London: Weidenfeld & Nicolson, 1968a).
Dahrendorf, Ralf, *Essays in the Theory of Society* (London: Routledge & Kegan Paul, 1968b).

Bibliography 147

Dean, Dwight G., 'Alienation and Political Apathy', in *Social Forces* xxxviii (1959–60) 185–90.

Donnison, D. V., and Plowman, D. E. G., 'The Functions of Local Parties: experiments in research methods', in *Political Studies*, ii (1954) 154–67.

Erbe, William, 'Social Involvement and Political Participation: a replication and elaboration', in *American Sociological Review*, xxix (1964) 198–215.

Etzioni, Amitai, *A Comparative Analysis of Complex Organisations* (New York: Free Press of Glencoe, 1961).

Eysenck, H. J., *The Psychology of Politics* (London: Routledge & Kegan Paul, 1954).

Gittus, Elizabeth, 'An Experiment in the Identification of Urban Sub-Areas', in *Transactions of the Bartlett Society*, ii (1963–4) 107–32.

Goldthorpe, John, and Lockwood, David, 'Affluence and the British Class Structure', in *Sociological Review*, xi (1963) 133–63.

Goode, Eriche, 'Class Styles of Religious Sociation', in *British Journal of Sociology*, xix (1968) 1–16.

Goodman, Leo A., and Kruskal, William H., 'Measures of Association for Cross Classifications', in *Journal of the American Statistical Association*, xlix (1954) 732–64.

Gordon, C. Wayne, and Babchuk, Nicholas, 'A Typology of Voluntary Associations', in *American Sociological Review*, xxiv (1959) 22–9.

Greer, Scott, 'Individual Participation in Mass Society', in *Approaches to the Study of Politics*, ed. Roland Young (Evanston: Northwestern University Press, 1958).

Gross, Neal, 'Social Class Identification in the Urban Community', in *American Sociological Review*, xviii (1953) 398–404.

Hartenstein, Wolfgang, and Liepelt, Klaus, 'Party Members and Party Voters in West Germany', in *Acta Sociologica*, vi (1962) 43–52.

Hausknecht, Murray, *The Joiners: a sociological description of voluntary association membership in the U.S.A.* (New York: Bedminster Press, 1962).

Himmelstrand, Ulf, 'A Theoretical and Empirical Approach to Depoliticization and Political Involvement', in *Acta Sociologica*, vi (1962) 82–110.

Hindess, Barry, 'Politics and Urban Structure: the case of the Liverpool Labour Party' (M.A. thesis, University of Liverpool, 1967a).

Hindess, Barry, 'Local Elections and the Labour Vote in Liverpool', in *Sociology*, i (1967b) 187–95.

Horton, John E., 'The Dehumanising of Anomie and Alienation: a problem in the ideology of sociology', in *British Journal of Sociology*, xv (1964) 283–300.

Jones, W. H. Morris, 'In Defence of Apathy: some doubts on the duty to vote', in *Political Studies*, ii (1954) 25–37.

Katz, Elihu, and Lazarsfeld, Paul F., *Personal Influence: the part played by people in the flow of mass communications* (New York: Free Press of Glencoe, 1955).

Kornhauser, William, *The Politics of Mass Society* (London: Routledge & Kegan Paul, 1960).
Kornhauser, William, 'Social Bases of Political Commitment: a study of liberals and radicals', in *Human Behaviour and Social Processes: an interactionist approach*, ed. Arnold M. Rose (London: Routledge & Kegan Paul, 1962).
Lane, Robert E., *Political Life: why people get involved in politics* (New York: Free Press of Glencoe, 1959).
Lane, Robert E., 'The Politics of Consensus in an Age of Affluence', in *American Political Science Review*, LIX (1965) 874–95.
Lapping, Brian, and Radice, Giles, eds., *More Power to the People: Young Fabian essays on democracy in Britain* (London: Longmans, 1968).
Lenski, Gerhard E., *Power and Privilege: a theory of social stratification* (New York: McGraw-Hill, 1966).
Lipset, S. M., *Political Man* (London: Heinemann, 1960).
Lipsitz, Lewis, 'Working Class Authoritarianism: a re-evaluation', in *American Sociological Review*, XXX (1965) 103–9.
Mayntz, Renate, 'Leisure, Social Participation and Political Activity', in *International Social Science Journal*, XII (1960) 561–74.
McClosky, Herbert, 'Conservatism and Personality', in *American Political Science Review*, LII (1958) 27–45.
McClosky, Herbert, 'Consensus and Ideology in American Politics', in *American Political Science Review*, LVIII (1964) 361–82.
McKitterick, T. E. M., 'The Membership of the Party', in *Political Quarterly*, XXXI (1960) 312–23.
Milbrath, Lester W., and Klein, Walter W., 'Personality Correlates of Political Participation', in *Acta Sociologica*, VI (1962) 53–66.
Milbrath, Lester W., *Political Participation: how and why people get involved in politics* (Chicago: Rand McNally, 1965).
Miller, S. M., and Riessman, Frank, 'Working Class Authoritarianism: a critique of Lipset', in *British Journal of Sociology*, XII (1961) 263–276.
Milne, R. S., and Mackenzie, H. C., *Straight Fight* (London: Hansard Society, 1956).
Moore, Barrington, Jnr, *Social Origins of Democracy and Dictatorship: lord and peasant in the making of the modern world* (London: Allen Lane, The Penguin Press, 1967).
Perrow, Charles, 'The Sociological Perspective and Political Pluralism', in *Social Research*, XXXI (1964) 411–22.
Plowman, D. E. G., 'Allegiance to Political Parties: a study of three parties in one area', in *Political Studies*, III (1955) 222–34.
Rogers, Everett M., *The Diffusion of Innovations* (New York: Free Press of Glencoe, 1962).
Rokkan, Stein, 'Electoral Activity, Party Membership and Organisational Influence: an initial analysis of data from Norwegian election studies, 1957', in *Acta Sociologica*, IV (1959) 25–37.
Rokkan, Stein, and Campbell, Angus, 'Citizen Participation in Political

Life: Norway and the U.S.A.', in *International Social Science Journal*, XII (1960) 69–99.

Rose, Arnold M., *Theory and Method in the Social Sciences* (Minneapolis: University of Minnesota Press, 1954).

Rose, Arnold M., 'A Comparison of Group Leaders and the Mass', in *American Sociological Review*, XXVII (1962) 834–8.

Rose, Arnold M., *The Power Structure* (New York: O.U.P., 1967).

Rose, Richard, *Politics in England* (London: Faber, 1965).

Rose, Richard, 'Class and Party Divisions: Britain as a test case', in *Sociology*, II (1968) 129–62.

Rosenberg, Morris, 'Test Factor Standardisation as a Method of Interpretation', in *Social Forces*, XLI (1962–3) 53–61.

Rothman, Stanley, 'Modernity and Tradition in Britain', in *Social Research*, XXVIII (1961) 297–317.

Runciman, W. G., 'Embourgeoisement, Self-Rated Class and Party Preference', in *Sociological Review*, XII (1964) 137–52.

Runciman, W. G., *Relative Deprivation and Social Justice* (London: Routledge & Kegan Paul, 1966).

Scott, J. C., Jnr, 'Membership and Participation in Voluntary Associations', in *American Sociological Review*, XXII (1957) 315–26.

Selvin, Hannan C., 'A Critique of Tests of Significance in Survey Research', in *American Sociological Review*, XXII (1957) 519–27.

Selznick, Philip, *The Organisational Weapon* (New York: Rand Corporation, 1952).

Shils, Edward A., *The Torment of Secrecy* (London: Heinemann, 1956).

Shils, Edward A., and Young, Michael, 'The Meaning of the Coronation', in *Sociological Review*, I (1953) 63–81.

Smith, David Horton, 'The Importance of Formal Voluntary Organisations for Society', in *Sociology and Social Research*, L (1966) 483–494.

Somers, Robert H., 'Measures of Association for Ordinal Variables', in *American Sociological Review*, XXVII (1962) 799–811.

Sorokin, Pitrim A., *Fads and Foibles in Modern Sociology and Related Social Sciences* (London: Mayflower and Vision, 1958).

Stacey, Margaret, *Tradition and Change: a study of Banbury* (Oxford: O.U.P., 1959).

Stark, Rodney, 'Class, Radicalism and Religious Involvement in Great Britain', in *American Sociological Review*, XXIX (1964) 698–706.

Stouffer, Samuel A., *Communism, Conformity and Civil Liberties* (New York: Doubleday, 1955).

Torgensen, Ulf, 'The Trend Towards Political Consensus: the case of Norway', in *Acta Sociologica*, VI (1962) 159–71.

Verba, Sidney, 'Organisational Membership and Democratic Consensus', in *Journal of Politics*, XXVII (1965) 467–97.

White, Winston, *Beyond Conformity* (New York: Free Press of Glencoe, 1961).

Wilensky, Harold L., 'Life Cycle, Work Situation and Participation in

Formal Associations', in *Ageing and Leisure*, ed. Robert W. Kleemier (New York: O.U.P., 1961).

Wright, Charles R., and Hyman, Herbert, 'Voluntary Association Memberships of American Adults: evidence from national surveys', in *American Sociological Review*, XXIII (1958) 284–94.

Zimmer, Basil G., and Hawley, Amos, 'The Significance of Membership in Associations', in *American Journal of Sociology*, LXV (1959–60) 196–201.

Index

Abrams, Philip, 44
Activists: political party, 45, 59–60; voluntary associations, 53, 58–60, 70–1, 79, 92–3, 98, 100, 101–3, 109, 114
Adorno, T. W., 83, 104
Agger, Robert E., 58
Alienation, 117, 119–20
Allardt, Erik, 23, 28, 54, 60, 81, 94
Almond, G. A., 54, 59
Anderson, Bo, 105
Anglicans, *see* Church membership
Anomie, 117, 119–20
Apathy, 24, 88, 96, 104, 119, 120–6, 131–3
Arendt, Hannah, 27, 65
Aron, Raymond, 129
Authoritarianism, *see* Political attitudes

Babchuk, Nicholas, 67
Banks, J. A., 12
Barker, Anthony, 133
Barnes, Samuel H., 54, 60, 76, 94, 104, 116
Bealey, Frank, 14, 27, 35, 42, 43, 52, 74, 83, 87, 95
Bell, Daniel, 18, 122
Bell, Wendell, 35
Benney, Mark, 14, 26, 42, 43, 47, 52, 74, 83, 87
Bettelheim, Bruno, 107–8
Birch, A. H., 42
Birnbaum, Norman, 130
Blondel, Jean, 14, 42, 47
Blumer, Herbert, 135
Boat, Marion D., 35
Bott, Elizabeth, 81
Bottomore, T. B., 26, 43, 51, 59
Bracey, H. E., 53
Bramson, Leon, 18, 117, 120

Campbell, Angus, 28, 88, 105
Canvassing, 47
Carter, Roy E., Jnr, 93
Cauter, T., 26, 59, 75, 94
Centers, Richard, 84
Chapman, Dennis, 76
Church attendance, 51–3
Church membership, 49–51, 52, 53, 61, 71–2
Church of England, *see* Church membership
Church ward, Liverpool, characteristics of, 34, 36–7, 38–40
Clarke, Peter, 93
Class, *see* Social class
Committee membership: political party, 45, 46; political clubs, 46; voluntary associations, 55–8. *See also* Activists
Community, 34, 80, 117–18, 129. See also *Gemeinschaft*
Conflict, 23–5, 62, 88, 113, 126–7, 131–3
Consensus, 18–19, 62, 101, 113, 117–19, 126–7, 129–33
Conservative clubs, 32, 45–6
Conservative Party membership, *see* Party membership, Activists
Correlation analysis, methods of, 136–40, 143–4
County ward, Walton, characteristics of, 35–6
Cross-cutting ties, 22–3, 61–2, 66, 72–3, 88, 113, 116, 130
Cross-pressures, 24, 95–6
Curtis, Richard F., 21–2

Dahl, Robert A., 53, 94, 96
Dahrendorf, Ralf, 11, 13, 18, 23, 25, 66, 81, 88, 104, 117, 126
Daily Express, 95
Daily Mail, 95

152 Index

Daily Mirror, 95
Dean, Dwight G., 119
Democracy: and conflict, 24–5; extremist politics, 126–7; participation, 13–14, 24, 104, 112, 120–5; social class, 65, 87; voluntary associations, 18–23
Dixon, K. F., 12
Donnison, D. V., 43, 85
Downham, J. S., 26, 59, 75, 94

Education: and authoritarian attitudes, 107–9; party membership, 73–5; voluntary associations, 18–23
Elections, 13, 35, 40, 125
Élites, 11, 120, 122
Erbe, William, 53, 119
Etzioni, Amatai, 125
Extremist politics, 24–5, 126–7, 130, 132–3

Fazakerley ward, Walton, characteristics of, 36
Finland, 28, 54, 60, 94
Folk society, 17, 19. See also Community, *Gemeinschaft*
Force, Maryanne T., 35
Functionalism, 18, 20

Gemeinschaft, 17, 117, 118, 129. See also Community
Germany, 13, 54, 104, 125
Gesellschaft, 117
Gittus, Elizabeth, 37
Goldthorpe, John, 82
Goode, Eriche, 49, 52, 71
Goodman, Leo A., 137
Gordon, C. Wayne, 67
Gradualism, 129–30
Gray, A. P., 14
Greer, Scott, 34, 118
Gross, Neal, 81

Happiness, politics of, 118–20, 124, 132
Hartenstein, Wolfgang, 54

Hausknecht, Murray, 26, 34, 52, 53, 54, 58, 75, 78–80, 90, 94
Hawley, Amos, 52
Himmelstrand, Ulf, 24, 88
Hindess, Barry, 12, 35, 39
Home tenure, 77–80
Horton, John E., 120
Housing, 35, 76–7
Hyman, Herbert, 75, 78

Ideology, 18, 110, 117, 119–20, 126
Industrial society, 17–18, 117, 120
Integration, 18–19, 78, 79–80, 87, 89, 112, 120
Interactionist sociology, 135–6, 144
Italian Socialist Party, 54, 60, 76, 94, 104, 116

Janowitz, Morris, 108
Japan, 125
Joiners, 59–60
Jones, W. H. Morris, 13, 122

Katz, Elihu, 91, 93
Klein, Walter W., 104
Kornhauser, William, 11, 18, 23, 25, 65, 104, 116, 117, 119, 121, 127, 131
Kruskal, William H., 137

Labour Clubs, 32, 45–6
Labour Party membership, *see* Party membership
Lane, Robert E., 18, 54, 91, 118
Lapping, Brian, 133
Lazarsfeld, Paul F., 91, 93
Lenski, Gerhard E., 66
Liberal Party membership, *see* Party membership
Liepelt, Klaus, 54
Lipset, Seymour Martin, 13, 24, 54, 90, 95, 108, 123, 124–5
Lipsitz, Lewis, 108, 124
Little, Alan, 44

Index

Liverpool, *see* Walton, Church ward
Liverpool Daily Post, 95, 96
Liverpool Echo, 95, 96
Lockwood, David, 82

McCann, W. P., 14
McClosky, Herbert, 105, 124
McKenzie, H. C., 95
McKitterick, T. E. M., 14, 47
Marxism, 65, 129
Mass communications, theory of, 93
Mass media, 89, 93–103, 114
Mass movements, 65, 121–2
Mass society, theory of, 11–12, 17–24, 34, 65, 110, 115–28, 135–6
Masses, 17, 120, 122, 124
Mayntz, Renate, 28
Michels, Robert, 20
Middle class: definition of, 38; self-assigned, 81–3, 86; and integration, 79–80; participation, 25–8, 70–2, 96, 115–16, 123, 133. *See also* Social class
Milbrath, Lester W., 24, 54, 75, 78, 80, 104
Miller, S. M., 124
Milne, R. S., 95
Monarchy, 101, 129–30
Moore, Barrington, Jnr, 125, 130

Nationalism, 130, 131
Newspaper readership, 94–103
Norway, 28, 54

Occupational class, 37–9, 67, 68–72, 83, 86–7, 108. *See also* Social class
Opinion leadership, 89, 90–3, 99, 100, 102
Ortega y Gasset, José, 121
Ostrom, Vincent, 58

Parsons, Talcott, 20
Partial correlation, 143

Participation, *see* Activists, Party membership, Voluntary associations
Party membership, *passim*: definitions, 31–3; sampling, 32–3; and activities, 42–7; church membership, 49–53, 61, 71–2; democracy, 13–15; education, 73–5; home tenure, 77–80; mass media, 95–8, 100–3, 114; opinion leadership, 92–3; political attitudes, 84–7, 106–9, 114; social class, 27–8, 68–72, 82–3, 115; trade unions, 48, 61; voluntary associations, 54–63, 79, 112, 114
Pear, T. H., 14
Perrow, Charles, 110, 115
Pesonen, Pertti, 28, 54, 94
Pirrie ward, Walton, characteristics, of, 36
Plowman, D. E. G., 43, 85
Pluralism, 62. *See also* Cross-cutting ties
Political attitudes, authoritarian, 89, 103–9, 114, 124; radical-conservative, 83–7
Political clubs, 32, 45–6
Political knowledge, 76
Political parties, *see* Party membership
Powell, Enoch, 131
Prejudice, 21–2, 104, 108
Pressure groups, 15–16, 123
Professional associations, 48

Radice, Giles, 133
Radio listening, 98, 99–103
Recruiting, party members, 14, 46, 47
Registrar-General, 37, 67
Religious identification and involvement, 49, 52
Religious organisations, *see* Church membership
Riesman, David, 117
Riessman, Frank, 124

154 Index

Rogers, Everett M., 93, 99
Rokkan, Stein, 28, 54, 91
Roman Catholic Church, 113. See also Church membership
Romanticism, 117
Rose, Arnold M., 19, 23, 26, 104, 117, 118, 143
Rose, Richard, 12, 14, 27, 116
Rosenberg, Morris, 141, 143
Rothman, Stanley, 129
Rousseau, Jean-Jacques, 129
Royal family, 101
Runciman, W. G., 38, 82

Sampling methods, 31–3
Scott, J. C., Jnr, 59, 78
Scottish Nationalism, 130, 131
Secondary associations, 17–18, 21–23, 117. See also Voluntary associations
Selvin, Hannan C., 136
Selznick, Philip, 117
Shils, Edward A., 24, 101, 130
Significance, statistical tests of, 136
Smith, David Horton, 20, 118
Social class: definitions, 66–7; self-assigned, 81–3, 86; socio-economic groups, 37–9, 68–9; and party membership, 68–72, 82–3; political attitudes, 86–7, 107–8; political participation, 25, 27–8, 35, 65, 115–16, 129; voluntary associations, 26–8, 67, 70–2. See also Middle class, Occupational class, Working class
Social control, 118
Social status, see Social class
Somers, Robert H., 138
Sorokin, Pitrim A., 84
Stacey, Margaret, 27
Standardisation, method of, 141–4
Stark, Rodney, 52, 71
Stouffer, Samuel A., 104, 107
Sun, 95

Television viewing, 98, 99–103
Tocqueville, Alexis de, 18

Tolerance, 21, 104, 107–8, 122
Torgensen, Ulf, 88
Totalitarian regimes, 118, 129
Trade unions, membership of, 47–8, 61

United States of America: church membership, 52–3, 71; consensus politics, 119, 132; home tenure, 78, 79; political participation, 53–4; politics and social class, 25, 28; voluntary associations, 16, 25–6, 53–4, 58–9, 75, 79, 94, 104
Urbanisation, 34, 35

Verba, Sidney, 23, 54, 59
Voluntary associations: committee memberships, 55–8; functions of, 18–23, 118; multiple memberships, 22–3, 61–3, 90, 103, 112–13; and church attendance, 52–3; education, 75–6; mass media, 94, 101–3; opinion leadership, 92–3; political attitudes, 104, 109; political participation, 15–17, 53–60, 123, 125, 133; social class, 26–28, 35, 67, 70–2; urbanisation, 34. See also Activists
Voting, 13, 24, 35, 40, 96, 125

Walton, Liverpool, characteristics of, 34, 35–40
Walton Conservative Association, 32, 44–5. See also Party membership
Walton Constituency Labour Party, 32, 44–5. See also Party membership
Warbreck ward, Walton, characteristics of, 36
Weber, Max, 67
Welsh Nationalism, 130, 131
White, Winston, 117
Whyte, William H., 117
Wilensky, Harold, 132

Working class: definition, 38; self-assigned, 81–3, 86; and authoritarian attitudes, 108, 124; integration, 87, 115; participation, 25–8, 70–2, 87, 96, 115–16
Wright, Charles R., 75, 78

Young, Michael, 101, 130
Young Conservatives, 32, 43, 44
Young Liberals, 32, 131
Young Socialists, 44

Zimmer, Basil G., 52

JN
231
.B48